THE IRISH JUDICIARY

Paul C. Bartholomew

Institute of Public Administration, Dublin, Ireland.

University of Notre Dame Press, Notre Dame, Indiana, U.S.A.

Published in Ireland for general distribution outside the
United States by the Institute of Public Administration,
57-61 Lansdowne Road, Dublin 4.

Published in the United States of America by the University
of Notre Dame Press, Notre Dame, Indiana 46556, U.S.A.

First published Autumn, 1971.

ISBN 0268-00457-9

Library of Congress Catalog Card Number: 70-175024

Printed by Mount Salus Press Ltd., Sandymount, Dublin.
Cover design by Murphy & Kyne, Dublin.

To My Friends in Ireland

PREFACE

The purpose of this study is to take a brief but reasonably thorough look at the judiciary of Ireland. Three aspects of the total picture are reviewed—the organization, jurisdiction, and procedure of the courts; a mildly behavioral investigation of the judges as persons; and a look at the law of Ireland with particular attention to constitutional law and, within that category, with emphasis on civil liberties. Some comparisons are drawn with United States law especially in the field of civil liberties and with particular attention to criminal prosecutions.

In the process of doing this study personal interviews were had with all judges of the three highest courts of Ireland appointed under the present Constitution of 1937, both sitting and retired, with two exceptions—one refused to be interviewed and the other died while the study was in progress. Of the thirty-five judges of the lowest court, seven were interviewed personally and ten returned a questionnaire. In addition to the judges, personal interviews were had with all living past holders of the office of Taoiseach, with President Eamon de Valera, former Minister for Justice Michael O Moráin, Attorney General Colm Condon, and others.

If credit were to be given to all those who assisted in this undertaking the litany of names would be long indeed. This presentation is the result of two semesters spent in residence in Ireland and, therefore, first credit should be given to those responsible in my home university for my being able to undertake the study. Among those should certainly be named the President of the University of Notre Dame, Rev Theodore M. Hesburgh, C.S.C., Rev John E. Walsh, C.S.C., Vice President for Academic Affairs, and Professor Stephen D. Kertesz, Chairman of the Committee for International Studies. In Ireland the co-operation and assistance received was little short of remarkable. Credit for this is due primarily to the efforts of the Chief Justice of the Supreme Court, the Hon. Cearbhall O Dálaigh. His numerous letters and phone calls to judges and others paved the way for success where otherwise there might well have been a fruitless venture. Among others to whom great appreciation is due must be mentioned Rev Professor Conor

Martin, Chairman of the Department of Ethics and Politics at University College, Dublin; Professor Roderick J. O'Hanlon, Professor of Constitutional Law and Professor John M. Kelly, Professor of Jurisprudence, both of University College, Dublin; Mr J. J. Donnelly and Mr Roger Hayes of the Department of Justice; Mr J. Kevin Waldron and Mr Michael Mellett of the Supreme Court Office, and Miss Catherine Noele Rafter, the Secretary of the Chief Justice of the Supreme Court; Mr G. D. Coyle, Secretary of the Bar Council and Mr Joseph Finnegan of the Incorporated Law Society. Many others should be mentioned but space limitations forbid.

Special mention should be made of Thomas E. Woods, III, General Counsel of the Michigan State Senate and Professor Andrew T. Smithberger of the University of Notre Dame who gave unstintingly of their time and talents. The contribution of the Celtic Legal Society of Chicago to the publication of this study certainly deserves particular mention. As with all of my work, my wife, Agnes, has been a real inspiration.

Note should be made of the fact that portions of Chapter One first appeared in an article of mine entitled "The Irish Judiciary" in the *Notre Dame Lawyer,* Volume 44, No. 4, April 1969, subsequently reprinted in *Administration,* the Journal of the Institute of Public Administration of Ireland, Volume 18, No. 3, Autumn 1970.

Paul C. Bartholomew

Dublin

March 1971

THE AUTHOR

Dr Paul C. Bartholomew is Professor of Government and International Studies at the University of Notre Dame. He has held visiting professorships at Northwestern University, Michigan State University, St Mary's College, Loyola University (Chicago), the University of Tennessee, the University of Chicago, and the National University of Ireland, Dublin. He has served as a consultant to the Department of the Navy, the U.S. House of Representatives, the State of Indiana, and the City of Chicago. He has been a visiting lecturer at the School of Public Administration, Dublin; Trinity College, Dublin; Queen's University, Belfast; University College, Galway; and Chulalongkorn University, Bangkok. He was a coordinator and principal lecturer at the Philippine Constitution Conference at Manila in 1970.

His publications include the following books: *A Manual of American Government*, *A Manual of Political Science Research*, *Public Administration*, *American Government Under the Constitution*, *Leading Cases on the Constitution*, *Profile of a Precinct Committeeman*, *The Indiana Third Congressional District*, *A Political History* and *Ruling American Constitutional Law* (two volumes). He has written a number of articles and reviews for various journals in the field including "Constitutional Law", 1956 and subsequent editions of the *Encyclopedia Americana*, as well as "Checks and Balances" and "Constitution" in the 1968 Edition. His annual analysis of the work of the Supreme Court appears in the December issue of the *Western Political Quarterly*. Among the other journals to which he has contributed are the *American Political Science Review*, *American Bar Association Journal*, *Notre Dame Lawyer*, *Midwest Journal of Political Science*, *Review of Politics*, *Journal of Politics*, *Federal Bar Journal*, *International Political Science Abstracts*, *Public Management*, *Social Science*, *New York State Bar Journal*, *Southwestern Social Science Quarterly*, *Traffic Quarterly*, *New Jersey State Bar Journal*, *Good Government*, *Police*, *Navy Management Review*, *Michigan State Bar Journal*, and *Illinois Municipal Review*.

TABLE OF CONTENTS

I

IRISH COURTS

I. Introduction

Apart from the native Brehon Law system, law and courts arrived in Ireland with the Normans in the twelfth century. Both systems co-existed outside the Pale for centuries until, with the ultimate defeat of the Irish princes, the English system was imposed throughout the whole of Ireland. However, the application of the benefits of English law was made available very tardily to the native Irish. Royal justice actually began to be dispensed about the beginning of the thirteenth century by a permanent deputy known as a Justiciar. From the use of royal writs by this representative of the King there was a gradual development into the jury system and assizes. In 1210 King John visited Ireland and ordered that English common law be used there. Initially this law was applied only to English settlers located chiefly around Dublin. Although application of the common law expanded as time went on, it was not until the seventeenth century that the native system of law, the *brehon*, was dropped completely, and English law was used throughout Ireland. By an Act of the Irish Parliament in the reign of James I in 1612[1] the English common law was applied to the whole of Ireland. 'All the natives and inhabitants of this kingdom without difference and distinction are taken into his Majesties gratious protection and doe now live under one law as dutiful subjects of Oour Sovereigne Lord and Monarch.'

II. Historical Development of the Irish Court System

The historical development of the first courts in Ireland paralleled the history of courts in England. The royal representative in Ireland was the Justiciar whose court before the end of the four-

teenth century came to be known as the Irish Court of King's
Bench. About the same time the courts of the Exchequer and
Common Pleas developed. Somewhat later the Court of Chancery
appeared. In time legislation provided for appointment of Justices
of the Peace and of Resident Magistrates. Over the years the Irish
Parliament enacted statutes by which English law was to be
applied in Ireland. This development was climaxed by the Act of
Union in 1800, enacted by both Irish and English parliaments,
which provided that the law and courts of Ireland as they then
existed should be continued, subject of course to later revision.
In fact, the Irish court system of 1800 was to undergo a basic
change in 1877 and then have little fundamental change until 1920.

The Irish judiciary in 1800 consisted of six types of courts, the
four courts already mentioned—Exchequer, Common Pleas, King's
Bench, and Chancery—plus the Court of Prerogative and Faculties
with probate jurisdiction (which was shortly to become the Court
of Probate) and the High Court of Admiralty. Between 1800 and
1877 three other courts were established. These were the Landed
Estates Court, the Court of Bankruptcy and the Court of Matrimonial Causes. Then in 1877 legislation was enacted which made
a basic change in the organization of the courts in Ireland. The
courts in existence were merged into one court — a very early
predecessor of the modern integrated court system. This court was
called the Supreme Court of Judicature in Ireland and had jurisdiction in law and equity. Within the court there were two divisions
— the High Court of Justice and the Court of Appeal. The former
had general original jurisdiction and also possessed limited appellate jurisdiction, specifically over cases coming from local courts.
Within the High Court the Landed Estates Court was merged with
Chancery, and the Court of Matrimonial Causes was merged with
Probate. Subsequent legislation moved all courts except Chancery
to Ireland's King's (Queen's) Bench Division.

In 1920 the revolutionary unicameral Dáil established a judicial
system of Parish courts with minor civil and criminal jurisdiction,
District Courts with greater (but still limited) civil and criminal
jurisdiction over Parish courts, Circuit Courts of unlimited civil
and criminal jurisdiction and a Supreme Court with both original
and appellate jurisdiction. These 'Dáil courts' were 'in competition
with' the regular courts that were still functioning ; they were
abolished by decree of the Provisional Government in 1922.

The 1922 Constitution of the Irish Free State contained a provision authorizing the establishment of a judiciary[2]. The Courts
of Justice Act of 1924 set up a system of courts consisting of a
unified District Court with minor civil and criminal jurisdiction,

and a Circuit Court of Justice with greater civil jurisdiction and unlimited criminal jurisdiction, excepting only murder, treason, piracy, attempted murder and conspiracy to murder[3]. The Circuit Court of Justice had appellate jurisdiction over cases heard originally in the District Court. The legislation also provided for a High Court of Justice with full civil and criminal jurisdiction and a Supreme Court of Justice with appellate jurisdiction. Finally, provision was made for a Court of Criminal Appeal consisting of judges from the High Court and the Supreme Court. Appeals could be taken from this court to the Supreme Court. The court organization thus established remained basically unchanged until the adoption of the Constitution of 1937.

In Ireland the judiciary is established by action of the Oireachtas[5] under authority conferred by Article 34 of the Irish Constitution. The court system must include, by constitutional mandate, courts of first instance and a court of final appeal. Further, the courts of first instance are to include a High Court which is to have complete original civil and criminal jurisdiction. By contrast, the United States Constitution empowers Congress to establish a Supreme Court and inferior tribunals. There is no constitutional direction with regard to the division of jurisdiction among these courts except that the original jurisdiction of the Supreme Court is limited to two kinds of cases — those involving states of the Union and those involving diplomats and consuls[6].

The constitutions both of the United States and of Ireland set up provisions for the judiciary in the respective countries and contain striking similarities in the language used[4]. However, one needs to remember the difference in the basic legal nature of the two political states. The United States is a federal republic and Ireland is a unitary republic. As a result, in the United States there are two governments existing side by side, federal and state, while in Ireland there is only one basic government with local governments serving in a subordinate administrative capacity in relation to the central government. As for the judiciary, this difference results in two distinct court systems in the United States while in Ireland there is one basic system. Obviously within this one system there may be all sorts of ramifications, such as separate arrangements for types of cases, *i.e.* civil and criminal, but the system is still under one government.

The courts of each of the states of the United States are established under the constitution and laws of each state acting independently and separately subject only to possible applicable federal statutes and constitutional provisions.

The Irish Constitution, like the American, empowers the national legislature to make exceptions to and regulations of the appellate jurisdiction of the Supreme Court, but in the Irish Constitution there is the proviso that none of these exceptions is to apply to cases involving the validity of a law under the Constitution. There is no such provision in the United States Constitution, and in the light of the Court's decision in *Ex parte McCardle*[7] the Court's jurisdiction in such matters may well be restricted by statute.

Under the Irish Constitution there is to be only one opinion by the Court in any case involving a question of the validity of a law under the Constitution that is, a post-1937 statute. The Constitution provides that

> The decision of the Supreme Court on a question as to the validity of a law having regard to the provisions of this Constitution shall be pronounced by such one of the judges of that Court as that Court shall direct, and no other opinion on such question, whether assenting or dissenting, shall be pronounced, nor shall the existence of any such other opinion be disclosed[8].

This rules out concurring opinions as well as dissenting opinions, very familiar features of the judicial scene in the Supreme Court of the United States[9].

The Courts [Establishment and Constitution] Act of 1961 proceeded to set up formally and officially in accordance with Article 34 of the 1937 Constitution the hierarchy of Irish courts as these courts exist today. These courts are the District Court, the Circuit Court, the Court of Criminal Appeal, the High Court, and the Supreme Court[10]. In point of actual fact, these courts were already in existence having been, as noted, established by the Courts of Justice Act of 1924 and had continued to function under Article 58 of the 1937 Constitution. This was a transitory provision under which the then-existing courts and judges were to continue to function until changed by statute. The 1961 Act, therefore, simply formalized under the new Constitution what was already a fact. In the same year there was also passed a Courts [Supplemental Provisions] Act which dealt with matters that under Article 36 of the Constitution were to be 'regulated in accordance with law'. Under this statute, incumbent judges who were willing to continue in office were to be the only ones qualified to be appointed as the first justices of these courts as new legal creations.

III. The Present Irish Judicial System

(A) The District Court

The lowest level of court in the system is the District Court[11]. Under Section 6 of the Adaptation of Enactments Act of 1922, the

District Justices were vested with all powers of Justices of the Peace or Resident Magistrates. Actually, 'District Courts' had been a part of the Irish judicial scene ever since 1920 when they had been established as a part of the programme of the revolutionary Dáil. These remained in operation until a decree of the 'cabinet of Dáil Eireann' abolished them on 26 October 1922[12]. On the same day a decree of the Minister for Home Affairs provided for the appointment of 'District Justices'. Later in the same year came the statute that conferred the powers of the Justices of the Peace and the Resident Magistrates on these District Justices. In the following year, 1923, the District Justices Act vested the appointment of District Justices in the Governor-General of the Irish Free State on the advice of the Executive Council. These District Justices continued to operate for another year, at which time the 'District Court' was established by the Courts of Justice Act of 1924. This arrangement continued through the adoption of the 1937 Constitution and until the 1924 plan was legally formalized under the new Constitution by the statute of 1961.

The District Court of Ireland is a unified court consisting of thirty-four justices and a President of the Court[13]. The country is divided into more than two hundred District Court Areas for the exercise of summary (criminal) jurisdiction and more than two hundred similar areas for the exercise of civil jurisdiction. These are then arranged into two groups of twenty-three District Court Districts each, one for civil jurisdiction and the other for criminal jurisdiction. The physical makeup of these Districts is not the same for these two types[14]. No jury is used in this court. Each of the justices holds court in his particular area. District Court judges, and all other judges as well, are appointed by the President of Ireland on the advice of the government. The number of judges on all of the courts is a matter for determination by statute[15]. The oath to be taken by all judges upon assuming office is specified in the Constitution[16]. It is basically the same as the English judicial oath pledging to do right 'without fear or favour, affection or ill-will towards any man . . . .' This declaration is made by the Chief Justice in the presence of the President of Ireland and by other judges in the presence of the Chief Justice in open court.

Barristers or solicitors who have actively engaged in the practice of law for not less than ten years are eligible for appointment to the District Court. Appointees to the Circuit Court must have been practising barristers for a minimum of ten years and those appointed to the High Court and the Supreme Court for twelve years, although the degree of 'practice' has at times been minimal.

The distinction between solicitors and barristers is recognized in the law. *Solicitors* constitute the lesser branch of the law and their legal recognition is based on a combination of training and examinations. In general, the solicitor deals with routine matters of the law. By contrast the *barristers* constitute the 'inner bar', although normally only senior counsel have this term applied to them. This distinction will be discussed in more detail later.

District Courts dispose of a fantastic number of cases each year. For example, in the year ending 31 July 1966 all of the District courts together disposed of a total of 322,080 cases. In the year ending 31 July 1967 the total was 340,501 ; in the year ending 31 July 1968, 357,797 cases ; in the year ending 31 July 1969, 380,597 cases ; and in the year ending 31 July 1970, 375,359 cases. These included both civil and criminal cases, children's court matters, and the enforcement of court orders and licences[17].

Under the terms of a 1946 statute,[18] District Court judges are given the same tenure as other judges, that is, they are not removable "except for stated misbehaviour or incapacity" and then only with a resolution passed by both houses of the Oireachtas[19]. In addition to removal, the 1946 legislation also provides for the disciplining of District Court Judges[20]. Under this provision the Minister for Justice may request the Chief Justice to appoint a judge to investigate the condition of health or the conduct of a District Judge and then report to the Minister for Justice. Under a more recent statute, the Courts Act of 1961, the Chief Justice may interview a justice of the District Court privately regarding conduct which the Chief Justice considers to be of a type that might bring the courts into disrepute. Finally, any judge can be removed by *address*, that is, by the President after a resolution of authorization has been passed by both houses of the Irish parliament, the Oireachtas.

It appears that no judge has actually been removed. One judge did retire after a motion for his removal for incapacity was put down. Judges of the High Court and the Supreme Court retire at seventy years of age, subject to exceptions, and judges of the Circuit Court also retire at seventy[21]. District Court justices retire at sixty-five but can get an extension year by year to the age of seventy. This annual extension is granted by a board consisting of the Chief Justice, the Attorney General, and the President of the High Court[22].

While there is nothing in the statutes as to the activities of a retired judge, there are restrictions set by regulation and tradition on a retired judge practising in a court at the level of which he was a judge. The General Council of the Bar of Ireland (commonly known as the Bar Council) has ruled on this on at least two separate occasions[23]. Under these rulings chamber (paper) work is proper but not actual court appearance. Thus a retired judge could not be an advocate but he could give advice or counsel. On the other hand, a retired District justice or Circuit Court judge could actually appear in the High or Supreme Courts. There have been a few instances of retired judges flouting the ruling. One District justice after retirement began to appear in the District Courts but after professional disapproval he desisted and retired from practice. Two former Circuit Court judges appeared in the Circuit Court. Apparently there would be no objection to practice by a retired judge of the High Court or Supreme Court.

As to the makeup of the *Bar Council,* it is composed of ten members of the Inner Bar (Senior Counsel) and ten members of the Outer Bar (Junior Counsel) elected for two-year terms which are staggered with one-half of the members being chosen each year. The Attorney General is also a member of the Council. Nominations are made very informally by means of a memo sent to the Secretary of the Council by a member other than the nominee and seconded by another member. Election is by secret ballot with only members of the Law Library voting. Almost all practising barristers are members of the Library.

(B) The Circuit Court

Next in the judicial hierarchy is the Circuit Court of Justice[24]. Technically there is only one District Court and only one Circuit Court, but the exercise of jurisdiction by particular justices and judges is in general confined to specified and limited geographical areas. Thus the Circuit Court is also an integrated court with nine judges and a President. The territory of Ireland is divided into eight circuits with a judge assigned to each. The ninth judge remains without permanent assignment being used in utility fashion. The judges of this court sit separately. As will be noted shortly, the District Court and the Circuit Court are both courts of limited jurisdiction. In the year 1965-1966 the Circuit Court disposed of a total of 13,688 cases. In 1969-1970 the total was 31,170 cases.

Ireland was originally divided into eight Circuit Court Circuits by the Courts of Justice Act of 1924 with one judge attached to each Circuit. By order made by the Government the number of Circuits was increased to nine as from the first of January 1938[25]. Two judges were assigned to the Dublin Circuit and one each to the eight provincial Circuits making a total of ten Circuit judges. The Circuits were then reduced in number to eight by an order effective as of 11 April 1960. This was done by amalgamating the

North Eastern and North Western Circuits and not interfering
with any others. Provision was also made for a reduction in the
number of judges from ten to nine on the occurrence of the first
vacancy. By the Courts Act, 1964, the number of judges was once
more increased to ten. This Act also authorized the Government to
alter at its discretion the composition of the Circuits except the
Dublin and Cork Circuits. In accordance with this an order of
25 August 1964 removed Sligo from the Northern Circuit and
added it to the Midland Circuit while removing Laois from the
Midland Circuit and adding it to the South Eastern Circuit. A
further order effective 1 January 1970 removed the County of
Wexford from the Eastern Circuit and added it to the South
Eastern Circuit. As a result the present Circuits are Dublin, Cork,
Northern (comprised of the counties of Cavan, Leitrim, Monaghan,
and Donegal), Western (comprised of the counties of Galway and
Mayo), Midland (comprised of the counties of Longford, Offaly,
Roscommon, Sligo, and Westmeath), Eastern (comprised of the
counties of Kildare, Louth, Meath, and Wicklow), South Western
(comprised of the counties of Clare, Kerry, and Limerick), and
South Eastern (comprised of the counties of Carlow, Kilkenny,
Laois, Tipperary, Waterford, and Wexford).

In connection with the organization of the courts two officers
should be noted. The *Commissioner for Oaths* is appointed by the
Chief Justice. He receives fees. He verifies affidavits and the
execution of certain documents. The *Notary Public* is also
appointed by the Chief Justice and he likewise is paid fees. His
function is to verify documents for international use.

(C) The High Court

The first court of general original trial jurisdiction in the Irish
system is the High Court[26]. Specifically mentioned in the
Constitution, this court is "invested with full original jurisdiction
in and power to determine all matters and questions whether of
law or fact, civil or criminal"[27]. This court succeeded the High
Court of Justice established under the Government of Ireland Act
of 1920 but this was a new court established pursuant to the
Constitution of the Irish Free State and was continued in both the
1922 Constitution and the 1937 Constitution. The present
organization of the High Court, and of the other courts, was set
by the Courts Act of 1961. The High Court consists of six ordinary
or *puisne* judges and an additional presiding judge who is known
as the President of the High Court. In addition to these seven
judges, the President of the Circuit Court is *ex officio* a judge of
the High Court but rarely sits as such. Normally the High Court

hears cases with the judges sitting singly, but when what amounts to a habeas corpus hearing is before the court, three judges sometimes sit on the case. At the discretion of the President of the High Court a divisional court of three High Court judges may be summoned to dispose of *state side matters*: habeas corpus, mandamus, certiorari, and prohibition[28]. When this court is exercising the criminal part of its jurisdiction it is known as the Central Criminal Court[29].

A jury may be used by the High Court in civil cases and must be used in criminal cases. In civil cases a vote of nine of the twelve jurors is sufficient to award a judgment, while in criminal cases the verdict must be unanimous. Statutory provisions governing the composition of juries are found chiefly in the Juries Acts of 1927 and 1945. Service on juries is limited to citizens between the ages of twenty-one and sixty-five who are registered voters and own property. Eligible women are not called unless they make application which is rare and then they are generally excluded by objection taken by one of the parties. Jurors Books which contain the names of eligible jurors in alphabetical order are prepared and maintained by County Registrars. When needed, jury panels are chosen by a form of random selection based on the frequency of occurrence of initial letter of surname. The empanelling and summoning of jurors is the responsibility of the Sheriffs or the County Registrars. In civil actions both the plaintiff and defendant may each challenge without cause not more than three jurors. In criminal trials the accused may challenge without cause not more than five jurors. This is what is known in the American judicial vernacular as peremptory challenge. Where two or more persons are accused together they may challenge without cause as many as ten jurors in cases of murder or treason and six in any other case. Challenges for cause are unlimited for both sides in both civil and criminal cases.

The jury system as presently administered leaves something to be desired. A Committee on Court Practice headed by Mr Justice Brian Walsh of the Supreme Court found in 1963 that fewer than 84,000 names were entered in the jurors books while by contrast the number in the electoral register at the same time was over a million and a half, a proportion of about one in twenty. The property qualification for jurors was first adopted because it was thought that men of property are more stable and less corruptible than men without property. Other criticisms of the jury system involve the absence of any fee or allowance for criminal trial jurors, the fact that the panels that are summoned are far too large and that jurors summoned are kept waiting unnecessarily.

The Attorney General can direct any juror not challenged by the defense to stand by without cause shown and any such juror is then not called for service until the remainder of the panel has been exhausted.

As to the business of the High Court, in the legal year of 1967-1968 there was a total of 558 cases, 470 of them jury cases and 88 non-jury; in 1968-1969 of 666 cases 550 were jury and 116 non-jury; and in 1969-1970 there were 586 jury and 96 non-jury for a total of 682 cases.

(D) The Court of Criminal Appeal

The Court of Criminal Appeal is an intermediate statutory court. First established by the Courts of Justice Act of 1924, the present court owes its existence to Section Three of the Courts Act of 1961. It is an *ex officio* court reminiscent of the Circuit Courts set up in the United States by the Judiciary Act of 1789[30]. The Court of Criminal Appeal consists of not fewer than three judges, one of whom is to be either the Chief Justice or a judge of the Supreme Court appointed by the Chief Justice. The other two are either two ordinary judges of the High Court appointed by the Chief Justice, or the President of the High Court along with a judge of the High Court named by the Chief Justice. However, any other judge or judges of the Supreme Court or the High Court may, at the request of the Chief Justice, attend as a member or members of the court. Invariably, the practice has been to limit the number of members of this court to three even though under both the 1924 and 1961 statutes there can be more than three. Although the Chief Justice is empowered by statute to direct it to sit elsewhere,[31] the court has always held its sessions in Dublin. As to its case load, in 1967-1968 the court handled fifty-three cases, in 1968-1969 it had thirty-seven cases, and in 1969-1970 the total was seventy-four cases.

(E) The Supreme Court

At the apex of the Irish judicial pyramid is the Supreme Court. This body consists of the Chief Justice (known also as the President of the Supreme Court) and four ordinary judges[32]. The President of the High Court may also serve as a member *ex officio*. Sessions are held in the Fourt Courts building in Dublin in four terms a year—Michaelmas from October to December, Hilary from January to March, Easter from April to May, and Trinity from June to July. The judges sit together for all cases, three judges constituting a quorum. In the 1965-1966 year the Court disposed of a total of 128 cases out of 250 on its docket at the beginning of that period. On 1 August 1969 the Court had ninety-four cases on the docket. By 31 July 1970 it had disposed of eighty-four, had sixteen cases standing for judgment, and 124 remaining on the docket.

The Supreme Court does not have administrative control over the lower courts but is able to make its views effective on lower court procedure by reversing cases in which the failure of the lower courts to follow the procedure suggested by the Supreme Court has amounted to error of law.

IV. Jurisdiction and Procedure

(A) District Court

Given this judicial structure, the next point of inquiry concerns the jurisdiction and procedure of these courts. The civil and criminal jurisdiction of the District Court is provided in the Courts Act of 1961[33]. Basically, the Act continued the jurisdiction that was vested in the District Court which had been established in 1924[34]. The District Court has a very limited civil jurisdiction. The limitation involves both the amount of money involved—in most instances a fifty or a hundred pound limit has been set—and the subject matter of a case. This court also has functions of a miscellaneous nature such as ordering payments from fathers of illegitimate children, enforcing court orders in debt cases, and issuing liquor and dance hall licenses. There is no equity jurisdiction vested in this court and it has no jurisdiction to determine questions of title to land. No jury is used in the District Court in civil cases, and appeals may be taken to the Circuit Court.

In the area of criminal jurisdiction the District Court hears what are called *summary* offenses, which are triable without a jury, and *indictable* offenses, which under the statutes may or must be tried by a judge and jury. These latter include all matters of statutory violation where no alternative remedy is provided. A distinction between summary and indictable offenses requires a look at the historical background involved. The procedures applicable to offenses triable by jury were reduced to statutory form in 1849 and 1851[35]. As a result, many offenses are both summary and indictable. While a large number of offenses which are indictable may be tried summarily, an accused person charged with an indictable offense has always had an absolute right to be tried by a jury. On the other hand, a person charged with a summary offense has no such right. A person who has been arrested must be taken 'as soon as may be' before either the District Justice or the *Peace Commissioner,* an official appointed by the Minister for Justice who serves without fees[36]. The Commissioner functions within a Garda District or Sub-District. This area may happen to span two counties.

Under present statutes, most of the work of the District Court is concerned with the trial of minor offenses which may be tried summarily. All but a few excepted indictable offenses may be tried by the District Court if the accused wishes to plead guilty[37]. The maximum punishment for offenses that are tried summarily by the District Court is a fine of one hundred pounds or imprisonment for twelve months, or both. The Attorney General may always object to a summary trial in the District Court and his consent is mandatory for the summary trial of certain offenses. In those cases where the mandatory consent of the Attorney General is not required, if the facts proved or alleged in a case really constitute a minor offense and if the accused does not object to being tried summarily the District Court may proceed to summary trial.

The grand jury was abolished in Ireland in 1924. In cases involving indictable offenses which do not qualify to be tried summarily in the District Court, the District Justice may conduct a preliminary examination at which prosecution witnesses are heard so that he may determine the existence of a prima facie case[38]. At the conclusion of this hearing, the justice may turn the accused over for trial on indictment either by the Circuit Court or the Central Criminal Court or he may discharge the prisoner. In the event of discharge, the Attorney General may overrule the District Justice and order the accused to be tried. This procedure is similar to the functioning of the United States Magistrate (formerly called the 'United States Commissioner') and the grand jury in the American federal court system. Newspapers may publish only the results of pre-trial hearings, not the evidence, unless the justice permits publication at the request of the accused[39].

(B) Circuit Court

The civil jurisdiction of the Circuit Court is not unlimited but is restricted to monetary values varying from sixty pounds to two thousand pounds, depending upon the nature of the case. For example, the lower figure holds in cases concerning the title to land and the higher figure applies to the administration of estates[40]. Juries may be used in civil cases in this court but seldom are. Furthermore, its jurisdiction extends to matters in equity as well as law.

The original criminal jurisdiction of the Circuit Court includes only indictable offenses[41]. Exceptions to this jurisdiction are treason, murder, conspiracy to murder, attempt to murder, and piracy which are tried in the High Court (the Central Criminal Court). Criminal cases may be transferred by a judge from one part of his circuit to another on application of either the Attorney General or the defendant, or a case may be transferred to the Central Criminal Court, possibly to avoid local prejudice. Cases in the Circuit Court are tried by a jury of twelve persons from the county in the Circuit in which the alleged offense was committed or in which the defendant has been arrested or resides. All jurors must be rated occupiers of property of a certain value as set by the Minister for Justice in the area of the court in question[42]. In exceptional cases a judge from another Circuit may be sent in, e.g., if the judge were a friend of the accused.

In both civil and criminal cases the Attorney General names one or more practising barristers to handle the cases in the courts. This man is chosen from a panel of available barristers made up of about ten seniors and about twenty or thirty juniors. The panel is larger in civil cases than it is in criminal cases. These men are paid at the discretion of the Attorney General and the work is usually very remunerative. This is referred to in the lawyer's vernacular as 'state work'[43]. Lawyers doing this do not work both prosecution and defense in the same term of court.

In each county there is a *state solicitor* who is paid by the state[44]. He normally handles cases arising in one county but may, if needed, move over to a case in another county. In criminal cases in Dublin the state solicitor from 'The Castle'[45] sends a brief of the case to the office of the Attorney General. This is then processed and sent back to 'The Castle'. At that point the Attorney General names a barrister to handle the case.

As to the probation system, at present a full-time Probation Service exists only in the Dublin Metropolitan District Court District where there are five Probation Officers attached to the Juvenile Court and one to the adult courts. This is obviously quite inadequate. In addition, one or two voluntary groups help the full-time officers in Dublin and there are also groups who provide a voluntary probation service for the courts in such larger centres as Cork, Limerick, and Waterford. There is also a Welfare Officer attached to Mountjoy Prison and another to St. Patrick's Institution for young offenders[46].

(C) High Court

The High Court has unlimited civil and criminal jurisdiction. In civil cases proceedings begin with the drawing up of a document by the plaintiff in which he states his claim. In pleadings in the High Court this document is called a 'Plenary Summons", a 'Summary Summons', a 'Special Summons' or a 'Petition' depending on the nature of the case. This is served on the defendant by a solicitor's clerk or other person and the defendant then answers. After the defendant's answer or 'appearance' the plaintiff sets out in detail his contentions in a 'Statement of Claim'. This is answered in a point-by-point reply by the defendant which the plaintiff may then attempt to controvert. These statements are all in writing and simply constitute a series of claims and denials—they do not deal with evidence. Depending on the nature of the case, the extended proceedings noted here are sometimes reduced to a simple claim and denial. The High Court also holds sessions on circuit when hearing civil appeals from the Circuit Court. In all cases the trial is before a jury[47].

As might be expected, criminal proceedings are initiated in much the same way as they are in the United States and England, except for the lack of the possibility of indictment by a grand jury. As noted earlier, when exercising its criminal jurisdiction, the High Court is known as the Central Criminal Court[48]. Its jurisdiction extends to all cases triable on indictment and is exercised by one (or, theoretically, more) judge designated by the President of the High Court. If two or more judges were so assigned they would sit together in collegial fashion, but in practice there are no collegial sittings. While the President of the High Court may direct the Central Criminal Court to sit anywhere, the court usually holds its sessions in the Green Street Courthouse in Dublin. In 1968 this court handled thirty-seven cases, in 1969 sixty-five cases, and in 1970 sixty-three cases.

What formerly were called the 'Prerogative Writs' (state side matters)—habeas corpus, certiorari, mandamus, quo warranto (no longer of any real significance), and prohibition—are now issued by any High Court judge and are directed to any of the inferior courts, but sometimes three judges sit in such matters. *Certiorari* is used primarily to determine improper exercise of jurisdiction by lower courts either in the sense of assuming excessive jurisdiction or breach of the rules or the requirements of natural justice such as bias in the exercise of jurisdiction. Certiorari will lie against any person or body exercising powers of a judicial nature. *Prohibition* is used principally to direct a lower court to refrain from exceeding or exercising its jurisdiction—an excess of legal power. *Mandamus* may be used against any person or body of persons to compel the carrying out of some duty imposed by law in an appropriate case.

V. Appellate Jurisdiction

(A) The Circuit Court

An appeal may be taken from the decision of a District Court in any case, but in criminal cases an appeal can be taken from the acquittal of an accused person only in very unusual circumstances, such as under the Fisheries Act[49]. Such actions are borderline actions between civil and criminal. Certain actions under spirits and illicit distillation acts are also pertinent here. The Circuit Court then holds a rehearing of the entire case and either the plaintiff or defendant may present new and additional evidence other than that used in the original hearing in the District Court. If instead of an appeal on the merits of the case in either a civil or criminal case there is an allegation that the District Court's order is defective in form, possibly beyond the court's jurisdiction, or contrary to natural justice, the more advantageous procedure is to apply to the High Court for a prerogative order of certiorari. Appeals from District to Circuit courts in criminal matters may usually be taken only on motion of the defendant, but in some instances determined by statute there may be appeal on the part of the complainant, as noted above. When hearing cases on appeal the Circuit Court does not use a jury and its decision is final, i.e., it is not subject to further appeal as a matter of right.

When an appeal from the District Court is based on alleged defects in form, i.e., when the question raised is whether that court has exceeded its powers, the appeal is not taken to the Circuit Court but to the High Court. Moreover, a District Judge may certify questions of law to the High Court; this is called 'case stated' procedure. If a District Justice refuses certification, either party may apply to the High Court for an order directing the District Justice to present the question of law. The High Court's action on questions such as these may be either to answer such question or questions or to reverse, affirm, or change in some manner the decision of the District Court.

(B) The Court of Criminal Appeal

As mentioned previously, when the High Court is exercising its criminal jurisdiction it is known as the Central Criminal Court. Cases tried on indictment in this court or in the Circuit Court may be appealed to the Court of Criminal Appeal. Only the accused in a criminal case may appeal to this court and appeal may be taken only if the defendant either secures a certificate from the trial judge or if the Court of Criminal Appeal directly grants leave to appeal. The overwhelming majority of such appeals is by the second method. The Courts of Justice Act of 1924 allows rather complete discretion to the Court of Criminal Appeal on the granting of appeal requests[50] but such requests are presumed to rest primarily on questions of law or situations where the trial in the lower court appears to have been unsatisfactory. The hearing in the Court of Criminal Appeal is based first on the trial record, but new or additional evidence may be heard. As a result of such hearing on appeal, the conviction may be affirmed, (particularly if the court feels, in spite of relatively minor points which could constitute reversible error, that there has been no injustice done) or reversed in whole or in part, or the sentence may be reduced or increased. Retrial of the accused may be ordered. The court's determination is final and may not be appealed except on certificate of the Court of Criminal Appeal itself or of the Attorney General. Although appeal can then be taken on such motion to the Supreme Court,[51] such appeals have been rare and cannot be taken if the conviction has been set aside by the Court of Criminal Appeal[52].

(C)　The High Court

The territory of Ireland is divided into a number of circuits for the High Court. Twice a year those judges 'ride circuit', hearing appeals in counties and county boroughs. Cases on appeal where there was no oral evidence in the court below are not heard on circuit but in Dublin as a matter of convenience to barristers and judges. Those heard on circuit will have a complete rehearing of the evidence even though a jury was used when the case was originally heard in the Circuit Court. In cases that are in the High Court on appeal from the Circuit Court either party in the case may ask the High Court to refer a question of law to the Supreme Court.

(D)　The Supreme Court

The appellate jurisdiction of the Supreme Court includes all matters commenced in the High Court as well as all those cases from the inferior courts that involve prerogative orders. The Supreme Court's appellate jurisdiction also includes, with certain reservations, 'case stated' matters coming from the Circuit Court and from the District Court by way of the High Court. In appeals to the Supreme Court the decision is made on the basis of the record in the trial court. The Supreme Court is free to make any decision that the trial judge (hearing the case *de novo*) might have made. This may involve reversal or complete change of the trial court's determination. Appeals from the High Court in cases in which a jury was used may bring a judgment from the Supreme Court ordering a new trial or vacating the trial court's verdict and substituting some other judgment. The average number of cases decided by the Supreme Court with full written opinion in a term would be about thirty-five. This is to be distinguished from cases disposed of without reserving judgment, that is, without waiting for a full written opinion. Some cases which are ready for hearing are always carried over from one term of the Supreme Court to the next. The number of these varies from term to term. For the 1970 Trinity term it was seventeen cases.

A majority of the judges questioned in this survey of all Irish courts (See Chapter Two) thought that the Supreme Court decides cases on 'merit' although there was some thought that there is a tendency to follow technicalities too closely or that even personal predilections might influence decisions although, of course, one is never quite sure to what extent, and critics may well be those whose decisions have been upset. Obviously a judge may have greater knowledge of a situation and decide a case differently than some of his colleagues. His particular experience before his appointment might influence his decisions. For example, a judge who has had considerable experience with clients in motor car cases might subconsciously favour a plaintiff in such cases before him later. One judge ventured the opinion that the judges on the Supreme Court, working on an intellectual and temperamental 'build', pick a conclusion and then argue to it. The Supreme Court has been accused of hair-splitting in favour of 'human rights', that if there is a legal 'loophole' the accused in a criminal case will be favoured. The Court has also been accused of being theoretical and impractical in its decisions, of being too inclined to ignore the judgment of a jury. It need hardly be mentioned in this connection that it is the duty of the court to set aside a jury's finding of fact if it is against the weight of the evidence or perverse or inconsistent or, in the case of damage, if the amount of the damages bears no reasonable proportion to the injuries.

On occasion a matter is decided by a judge, regardless of the level of the court, in a way that causes some to question his objectivity. For example, a prominent Catholic Judge had two child custody cases before him. In the first case the father of the child was a Catholic and the mother a non-Catholic. The judge gave the father custody of the child. In the second case the mother was a Catholic and the father was not. This time the mother was given custody of the child. Other factors may well have influenced the decisions but to some persons it looked as though religion was the determining factor. However, here note should be taken of the principle of law applicable to child custody cases, that is, the welfare of the child, and an important factor in that welfare is the

religion of the child. In Ireland a mixed marriage usually means
that the children will be brought up as Catholics (ne temere decree)
and it is thus to be expected that the Catholic parent (other things
being equal) will be awarded the custody of the child.

VI. Judicial Review

Judicial review is specifically provided by the terms of the
Constitution which states that:

> The jurisdiction of the High Court shall extend to the
> question of the validity of any law having regard to the
> provisions of this Constitution, and no such question shall
> be raised (whether by pleading, argument or otherwise) in
> any Court established under this or any other Article of
> this Constitution other than the High Court or the Supreme
> Court[53].

It is maintained by some that Mr. Eamon de Valera and others
concerned with the writing of the 1937 Constitution did not intend
to vest in the courts any power of review analogous to that
exercised by the Supreme Court of the United States. In fact,
however, judicial review in Ireland is quite analogous to that in the
United States[54]. The power was first exercised in 1939 and has
been exercised on several subsequent occasions[55]. As noted earlier,
when the Supreme Court is ruling on a question as to the validity
of a law having regard to the provisions of the Constitution, the
decision is to be pronounced by only one judge of the Court and
there are to be no other opinions either concurring or dissenting[56].
This is known as the 'one judgment' rule. As the words of the
Constitution indicate, neither the District Court nor the Circuit
Court has jurisdiction to hear cases questioning the validity of a
statute under the Constitution[57]. This is a distinct difference from
the situation in the United States where Article VI of the Constitution expressly makes the Constitution binding in all matters
before any of the courts, state and federal. In Ireland the net result
is that the inferior courts must in all instances regard all post-1937
statutes as constitutional[58]. The only departure from this occurs
when a superior court has before it the question of the constitutionality of a statute in issue in a lower court. The lower court may
then await action by the superior court on the matter before acting
itself[59].

The Supreme Court has expressly declared that it will not adhere
to stare decisis in rendering its decisions[60]. Two reasons have been
advanced for this. First, the courts established under the present

Constitution are 'new' courts and should not be bound by the decisions of previous courts. Second, the 'one judgment' rule suppresses minority opinions and the very real possibility that these might gain favour in later years militates against taking prior judgments as 'law'[61].

The Supreme Court has established the rule[62] that a statute enacted since 1937 (the date of the current Constitution) is to be presumed valid until the contrary is clearly shown. Thus, the burden of proof of the unconstitutionality of a statute is on the party challenging the statute.

There are two points of distinction that should be noted in regard to a declaration of inapplicability of a law passed before or after the Constitution of 1937. The first point involves a matter of semantics. A law passed before the Constitution of 1937 is said to be 'inconsistent'[63] while those passed afterwards are said to be 'repugnant' to the Constitution. A second point is that in such decisions of the Supreme Court involving pre-1937 legislation there may be a dissenting opinion or opinions but for laws enacted since that time there is to be only a single opinion of the Court.

While the provisions of the Constitution[64] that the High Court and the Supreme Court may exercise jurisdiction to determine constitutionality only in respect to laws already existing preclude the possibility of advisory judicial opinions (such as are sometimes found on the state level in the United States[65] but not on the federal level),[66] there is the possibility of an advance determination of the constitutionality of proposed legislation. The Constitution provides that the President may, after consultation with the *Council of State*,[67] refer to the Supreme Court for a determination of the constitutionality of any bill, or any specified provision or provisions of a bill, passed by both houses of the Oireachtas[68]. Exceptions to this provision are made for 'a Money Bill, or a Bill expressed to be a Bill containing a proposal to amend the Constitution, or a Bill the time for the consideration of which by Seanad Eireann shall have been abridged . . .'[69] This procedure of securing an advance determination of constitutionality has been employed three times since 1937[70].

In the area of judicial review, it has been said that the courts of the United States can make law but that the Irish courts can unmake law. This is an oversimplification but there is some validity to the statement. As noted, under the Irish Constitution the President has the right to refer bills presented to him after passage by both Houses of the Oireachtas to the Supreme Court for opinion as to constitutionality[71]. It is said that President de Valera after 1939 thought of having a separate court established to deal with constitutional issues. He was disturbed by the decision of the High Court in 1939 in the case involving the Offences Against the State Act. The Supreme Court refused to review this High Court decision by refusing to entertain an appeal from an order absolute of habeas corpus. While the Act was not declared unconstitutional, the word 'satisfied' in the Act was held to require a judicial inquiry before internment could be ordered. An amending Bill substituted the test of 'opinion' and the Supreme Court, on a reference, upheld the constitutionality of the internment provisions of the Bill.

Many rights guaranteed in the Constitution cannot be deprived 'save in accordance with law'[72]. Thus the chief question the courts have to answer frequently is whether laws have been properly enacted, the constitutional inquiry therefore being primarily of procedural matters rather than substantive. However, this is not the whole of the picture since 'in accordance with law' has been interpreted to mean *in accordance with the law of the Constitution* and this brings up a substantive issue[73].

Under the Constitution[74] the legislature has the right to pass any law that 'is expressed to be for the purpose of securing the public safety and the preservation of the State' during a time of declared emergency. The constitutional validity of such laws cannot be questioned. In 1939 an emergency was declared that has not been terminated. The resolution is still on the parliamentary record. However, there is no legislation on the statute books which rests on this resolution for its validity. To do so such an act would need to bear the 'label' of 'emergency legislation' or 'emergency in war'[75].

On the matter of the relations of the judiciary with the executive and legislative branches of the government, only a small minority of the judges questioned in our survey of all courts thought that the executive and legislative branches are critical of the judiciary. Where there have been reversals of Supreme Court decisions on legislation by subsequent legislation most of those who answered this question thought that this occurred only for the purpose of curing the 'vice of vagueness' found in the voided statutes by the Supreme Court. Also loopholes have been closed in revenue and road traffic acts. By way of example of changes in statutes brought about by interpretation of a statute by the Supreme Court, an act was passed in 1949 to amend the 1947 Finance Act. The Court had decided that the 1947 Act did not apply to purchase by way of lease, therefore the act was changed so that it would apply. In another instance, the Court in interpreting an old act that had been passed under British rule in the 18th Century and carried over into effect under the Republic held that there was no liability for fires escaping property except in case of negligence. This statute applied to a dwelling house but not to a factory. In the Accidental Fires Act of 1943 this was changed to include factories[76]. Another example of such legislation was the Emergency Powers Act of 1940 during World War II. Also there was the amendment in 1965 of the Civil Liability Act. By contrast the 1961 decision on electoral districts was adhered to even though it was disliked[77]. After the decision in the Modern Homes, Ltd. case[78] a new and comprehensive town planning act was passed after some delay[79].

Compliance with decisions of the courts seems to be no problem for judges but of those who answered in the survey almost half had been forced at one time or another to hold persons in contempt for refusal to comply with determinations of their courts. This relatively minor difficulty was found to a greater or lesser degree on all court levels.

The judges overwhelmingly feel that relations with the press are good. Very few complained of inaccurate reporting. Some thought that the press in general, and particularly law reviews, are not sufficiently critical. In the Republic there are really only three law reviews, the *Irish Law Times*, the *Irish Jurist*, and the *Dublin University Law Review*. Mention should also be made of the Queen's University of Belfast law review, the *Northern Ireland Legal Quarterly*.

VII. The Legal Profession

In Ireland as in England the legal profession is divided into two branches, solicitors and barristers. Less than one-fifth of the practising lawyers are barristers, which means that the solicitors bear the brunt of the burden of the efficient administration of justice. Until well past the middle of the nineteenth century all solicitors were members of the Honorable Society of King's Inns. Whatever there was in the way of legal education at this time was under the supervision of this body. Actually rather than educating persons for the profession of law what the body did was to set rules for the admission of persons to learn. The class of legal practitioners known as 'solicitors' today developed in both England and Ireland from three groups, the clerks of barristers, persons appointed by judges to serve as court officials and known as 'attorneys', and the 'proctors' of the Admiralty and Ecclesiastical courts. As a result of legislation in 1866 and in 1898 complete disciplinary power over the solicitors' profession was given to the Incorporated Law Society of Ireland. Ultimately the President of the High Court determines such matters subject to appeal to the Supreme Court[80].

The system of legal education in Ireland is rigidly controlled by statute and responsibility for this for solicitors is now divided between the Law Society, the universities, and the solicitors to whom the candidates for the law are apprenticed. At this point the student is really an office clerk for the solicitor, a privilege for which the student sometimes pays a substantial fee. The basic legal education at the present time is a combination of practical training as an apprentice to a solicitor and examinations. How 'practical' this arrangement is remains a question in the light of the way the system works. To be admitted to apprenticeship the individual must be at least seventeen years of age and have passed the preliminary examinations of the Incorporated Law Society. The expiration of the time spent as an apprentice normally runs concurrently with the time during which he is taking his examinations. The apprenticeship period is set at five years but this can be reduced to four years if the candidate takes a university degree. During the time of apprenticeship the candidate takes two years of lecture courses in law at a university and at the Incorporated Law Society, and also takes three law examinations and two examinations in the Irish language. The law examinations are administered by the Law Society which has quarters at the Four Courts. During the term of his apprenticeship the candidate may elect to take a university degree in law. A little less than half of the apprentices do this. He then applies to be admitted to the roll of solicitors. Given this programme, including time taken for study for examinations, there is some question as to how much time the apprentice has been able to spend in acquiring any real acquaintance with the practical aspects of a solicitor's work.

In general the work of a *solicitor* is that of routine matters of law. However, the scope of a solicitor's work has broadened greatly in recent years. Ordinary commercial matters, probate, the making of wills, and preparing cases for litigation are still very much a part of his work but areas of specialty have opened up especially in the areas of taxation and company law where modern solicitors are acquiring an expertise that is much sought after. Solicitors have the full 'right of audience' in the Circuit and District courts, and it has been proposed that this be extended to the superior courts as well. Many solicitors do not exercise their right of audience but instead brief counsel, particularly in the Circuit Court, to plead their clients' cases.

By contrast, *barristers* constitute 'the Bar' and are referred to as 'counsel'. They are divided into two groups, junior and senior, with the latter known as the 'Inner Bar' and the former as the 'Outer Bar'. Barristers plead cases—have the 'right of audience'—

before the higher courts and admission to this status is regulated by the Benchers of the King's Inns. This in a sense is a 'legal university'. Courses of lectures by professors in universities and later by professors appointed on a part-time basis by the Inns must be taken by candidates for call to the bar after which they must pass examinations in both law and the Irish language. The full period of four years for this for a non-university student (one not proceeding to a degree) may be reduced to three years for those who have or are proceeding to university degrees, but then the degree must be taken before admission to the degree of Barrister-at-Law (B.L.). Having done these things and having dined at the Inns a prescribed number of times the candidate is called to the Bar. Upon admission a new barrister usually spends the first year or so as an understudy of an older barrister. Then his solicitor friends will recommend clients for him. If they do not, he may be forced to leave law and try something else or be able to use his law training with a company or corporation. A barrister is always on his own. Law firms on the American model are not found in Ireland. Solicitors may form partnerships but barristers may not. The older and more eminent barristers may be admitted to the ranks of 'senior counsel'. Call to the Inner Bar is by recommendation of the Chief Justice and the Attorney General. This is known as 'taking silk'. Applications for this are cleared with the Government. This is known as *Patent of Precedence*. The holder of the Patent is then called to the Inner Bar by the Chief Justice. He can then for the first time sit in the front bench of those reserved for barristers in court.

The senior members of the legal profession, called 'Benchers', exercise discipline over the Bar, but there is a separate body called the General Council of the Bar or simply the Bar Council. As noted earlier, this body is democratically elected by secret ballot by all practising barristers and is composed of both junior and senior counsel. By contrast the Benchers are self-perpetuating, in effect filling vacancies in their own ranks. The Benchers of the Honourable Society of the King's Inns control entry to the profession, determine the educational syllabus, conduct the final examination, admit to the degree of Barrister-at-Law, and have power to disbar a barrister guilty of unprofessional conduct. In a word, the primary concerns of the Benchers are to educate students for the Bar and then to maintain the traditions of the profession. Among the Benchers, in spite of the 'senior' atmosphere, there are some members of the junior bar. The Benchers consist of Bar Benchers and Judicial Benchers, the former being elected by the Benchers when a vacancy occurs and the latter holding office by virtue of being judges of the High Court or the Supreme Court.

From what has been said it is probably obvious that it is not normal for one to be a solicitor before becoming a barrister or vice versa. As a matter of fact the very arrangement militates against this. At the present time, at least in theory, neither a barrister nor a solicitor can move to the other branch without a substantial waiting period generally involving the taking of further examinations to enable him to qualify for the other branch of the profession. The cooperation of the Incorporated Law Society can expedite the process. In the case of a transfer from the solicitor's profession to the Bar, a solicitor is required to pass six months 'in limbo' with all connections with the solicitors' profession being severed.

There is much to be said for the system of training barristers and solicitors. It engenders comaraderie, since all study together in one room. The communal life of the barristers has been credited with leading to the high ethical standards of the Irish legal profession. However, it is felt by some that the Irish legal education is too narrow in that it does not embrace enough social science. Also Ireland lacks the academic criticism which would come from full-blown law schools although the University Law Schools, where the greater part of the training of lawyers is conducted, have an increasing number of full-time teachers. Almost all Irish lawyers do have a general educational background rather than a specialty.

VIII. The Cost of Litigation

In civil cases parties to the litigation pay court fees, the expense of having witnesses, and other expenses in connection with the gathering of evidence as well as the fees charged by the litigant's own counsel. In a civil action the successful party may bill the loser for these party-and-party 'costs' including so much of the solicitor fees and expenses as may be allowed by a court official known as the *Taxing Master*. If the loser disagrees as to the amount, the matter can be appealed to the Taxing Master, whose decisions in turn can be appealed to a judge of the High Court. All of this 'taxation of costs', of course, involves added expense. The legal profession sets minimum fees for barristers and the fees for solicitors are set by statute for routine matters such as conveyancing, but for services related to litigation and court work there are no fixed charges either for solicitors or barristers.

Under the Criminal Justice Act of 1962, indigent persons in criminal cases are entitled to necessary legal assistance at government expense. In civil cases, litigants without funds are extended aid by the legal professsion if trade union aid or insurance coverage is not available[81].

There is no formal connection between the Minister for Justice and the *Attorney General*. The latter is really the Taoiseach's man in the sense that while he is an independent constitutional officer, he is appointed by the Taoiseach and may be required to resign by the Taoiseach, but he does work informally with the Ministry of Justice and other departments on legal matters. The Attorney General sits with the Cabinet but he does not vote. Proposed legislation is worked out in regard to legal points with him. Further the Attorney General may give an interpretation of the Constitution or a statute for a particular officer but there is no publication or general circulation of this and the courts do not cite this opinion. The function of representation of the government in cases before the Supreme Court that in the United States is lodged with the Solicitor General is with the Attorney General in Ireland, but, although there is no rule against it, he never personally appears in court[82]. He has a permanent staff of barristers to assist in the technical work of his office. They are civil servants. It is entirely permissible for the Attorney General to carry on a private practice of law while holding office.

IX. Conclusion

While the similarities in judicial organization and procedure in Ireland and the United States are perhaps to be expected in the light of history, the parallels are nevertheless mildly impressive. The systems themselves are different because of the difference in basic governmental principles—federal and unitary—but in each country the legislature, Oireachtas and Congress respectively, has great power over the structuring of the judicial system and, to a lesser extent, the jurisdiction of the courts. There is an express provision for judicial review in the Irish Constitution; in the United State's Constitution the power has a basis in the combination of Article III, Section Two, with Article VI. However, in both countries the realization of the power has been the result of historical development. The names of the courts are familiar with only an exception like 'High Court' to attract attention. Although differences exist between the two systems, as, for example, the fact that the Irish Supreme Court in considering the constitutionality of a post-1937 statute, has no concurring or dissenting opinions, such differences are minor. There seems to be no escape from the conclusion that the similarities in the two systems outweigh the differences. This may be regarded as another of the ties that bind the Irish and American peoples.

APPENDIX A

Organization of the Courts of Ireland

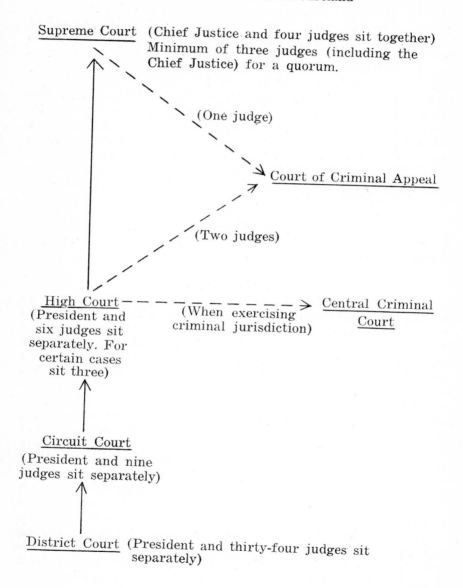

Supreme Court (Chief Justice and four judges sit together) Minimum of three judges (including the Chief Justice) for a quorum.

(One judge)

Court of Criminal Appeal

(Two judges)

High Court — — — — — — — — — → Central Criminal Court
(President and six judges sit separately. For certain cases sit three) (When exercising criminal jurisdiction)

Circuit Court
(President and nine judges sit separately)

District Court (President and thirty-four judges sit separately)

REFERENCES

1. 11/12/13 James I, Chap. V (1612), Sect. 5. It was entitled "An Act of Repeale of diverse Statutes concerning the Natives of this Kingdom of Ireland."
2. Constitution of the Irish Free State, Art. 64.
3. Courts of Justice Act, 1924, Sect. 49.
4. Constitution of Ireland, Art. 34; Constitution of the United States, Art. III. Unless otherwise noted, this and subsequent references to the Irish Constitution are to the 1937, the current, Constitution.
5. The Oireachtas is the name given to the combination of the President and the Houses of the Irish Parliament of which the Dáil is the House of Representatives and the Seanad is the Senate. The Constitution of Ireland provides in Article 15 (1) that "The National Parliament shall be called and known, and is in this Constitution generally referred to as the Oireachtas.
   "The Oireachtas shall consist of the President and two Houses, viz. a House of Representatives to be called Dáil Eireann and a Senate to be called Seanad Eireann."
6. U.S. Constitution, Art. III, Sect. 2.
7. Wallace 506, 1868.
8. Article 34 (4), (5). This type of reference to the Irish Constitution 'translates' as Article 34, Section 4, Subsection 5. This type of constitutional reference will be used hereafter.
9. However, if a question should arise as to whether a law in force in Saorstát Eireann immediately prior to the coming into operation of the 1937 Constitution is 'consistent' with this Constitution then dissenting opinions are permissible.
10. The establishment of the Court of Criminal Appeal is not thought to have been provided for by the Constitution.
11. See Appendix A, *supra*, this chapter.
12. V. T. H. Delany, *The Administration of Justice in Ireland*, p. 39.
13. Courts (Supplemental Provisions) Act, 1961, Sect. 32.
14. The makeup of these areas and districts can be changed by order of the Minister for Justice under the Courts of Justice Act, 1953 (No. 32 of 1953), Sections 22 and 26. Note, for example, District Court Districts (Dublin) (Amendment) Order, 1970.
15. Irish Constitution, Art. 36 (1), (2).
16. Irish Constitution, Art. 34 (5), (1, 2, 3, 5).
17. District Court records, Department of Justice. Statistics of other courts are also from the Department of Justice or the Supreme Court Office.
18. Courts of Justice (District Court) Act of 1946. See also Delany, *supra*, p. 66.
19. Irish Constitution, Art. 35, (4), (1).
20. Courts of Justice (District Court) Act of 1946, Sect. 21.
21. Courts of Justice Act, 1961, Sect. 18 (1).
22. Courts of Justice Act, 1936, Sect. 49; Courts of Justice Act, 1961, Sect. 30 (1).

23. Rulings of the Bar Council, May 12, 1944, February 26, 1968.
24. Courts (Establishment and Constitution) Act of 1961.
25. Circuit Court (New Circuits) Order, 1937 under Courts of Justice Act, 1936, Sect. 13.
26. Courts (Establishment and Constitution) Act of 1961.
27. Irish Constitution, Art. 34 (3), (1).
28. Irish Constitution, Art. 40 (4), (2 and 4).
29. Courts (Supplemental Provisions) Act of 1961, Sect. 11 (1), (2).
30. Judiciary Act of 23 September 1789, 1 Stat. 73.
31. Courts of Justice Act of 1924, Sect. 28.
32. Courts (Establishment and Constitution) [No. 38] Act, 1961, Sect. 1 (2). If the Chief Justice is not present then the senior judge present presides, seniority being determined by the date of appointment to the Supreme Court. Since the President of the High Court ranks as a judge of the Supreme Court and second in precedence to the Chief Justice, in the absence of the Chief Justice, if the President of the High Court were sitting, he would preside.
33. Courts (Supplementary Provisions) Act of 1961, Sect. 33.
34. Courts of Justice Act of 1924, Sect. 67.
35. Indictable Offenses [I.R.] Act of 1849; Petty Sessions [I.R.] Act of 1851.
36. Criminal Justice Act, 1951, Sect. 15.
37. Criminal Procedure Act, 1967, Sect. 13.
38. Actually no witnesses may be heard, but statements of their evidence and other documents may be read. See Criminal Procedure Act, 1967 [No. 12], Part II.
39. Criminal Procedure Act, 1967, Sect. 17 (3).
40. Courts of Justice Act of 1924, Sect. 48; Courts (Supplemental Provisions) Act of 1961, Sect. 22. The civil jurisdiction of the Circuit Court in contract and tort is limited to six hundred pounds. In cases involving title to lands the Circuit Court has jurisdiction, provided the Poor Law valuation of the land does not exceed sixty pounds. A property with a Poor Law valuation of sixty pounds would, however, be worth ten thousand pounds or more. In equity proceedings generally the Circuit Court has jurisdiction provided the Trust Estate does not exceed two thousand pounds or, insofar as it consists of lands, if the rateable valuation does not exceed sixty pounds. For details see the Third Schedule to the Courts (Supplemental Provisions) Act, 1961.
41. Courts (Supplemental Provisions) Act of 1961, Sect. 25.
42. Juries Acts, 1927 and 1945, Sect. 3 (1).
43. This is to be distinguished from 'state side' work a term used to describe work in connection with applications relating to habeas corpus, certiorari, prohibition, mandamus, quo warranto, and bail motions.
44. The Chief State Solicitor (in Dublin) is a civil servant and so also are the solicitor members of his staff. The other (county) state solicitors hold a permanent retainer which excludes them from criminal practice, but they freely carry on civil practice.
45. 'Dublin Castle', formerly British administrative headquarters, now contains, among others, the State Solicitor's offices.

46. Report of the Minister for Justice furnished to the author.

47. Courts of Justice Act, 1936, Sect. 34 (2).

48. Courts of Justice Act, 1924, Sect. 3; Courts (Supplemental Provisions) Act of 1961, Sect. 11 (1), (2).

49. Fisheries (Consolidation Amendment) (No. 14 of 1959) Act, 1959, Sect. 310.

50. Courts of Justice Act of 1924, Sects. 32, 33, and 97.

51. Courts of Justice Act of 1924, Sect. 29.

52. See *The People* (A.-G.) v. *Kennedy*, 1946 I.R. 517.

53. Irish Constitution, Art. 34 (3), (2).

54. John M. Kelly, *Fundamental Rights in the Irish Law and Constitution*, pp. 17-19.

55. *Ibid.*, pp. 25-26.

56. Irish Constitution, Art. 34 (4), (5). See Footnote 9 *supra*.

57. A litigant in such a case would not be without remedy. He could move the High Court for an order of prohibition to prevent the Court hearing the charge, or, if convicted, he could move to quash on certiorari.

58. As to statutes enacted prior to the coming into operation of the present Constitution, see *The State* (*Sheerin*) v. *The Governor of St. Patrick's Institution and the Attorney General*, 1966 I.R. 379.

59. *The State* (*A.-G.*) v. *Mangan*, 1961 I.R. 17.

60. *The State* (*Quinn*) v. *Ryan*, 1965 I.R. 70; 100 I.L.T.R. 105. *Attorney General* v. *Ryan's Car Hire*, 1965 I.R. 642; 101 I.L.T.R. 57.

61. Kelly, *op. cit.*, footnote 54, pp. 30-33.

62. *In re Article* 26 *and the Offences Against the State* (*Amendment*) *Bill*, 1940, 1940 I.R. 470.

63. Irish Constitution, Art. 50 (1).

64. Irish Constitution, Art. 13 (3); Art. 34 (3), (2).

65. E.g., Florida Constitution, Art. 4, Sect. 13; Massachusetts Constitution, Chap. III, Sect. 83.

66. *Muskrat* v. *United States*, 219 U.S. 346, 1911.

67. The Council of State is a body composed of seven persons who can be classified as *ex officio* members, that is, persons who have held the offices of President, Taoiseach, Chief Justice, or President of the Executive Council Saorstát Eireann, and 'Such other persons, if any, as may be appointed by the President . . .' Irish Constitution, Art. 31 (2). However, no more than seven of the President's nominees may be on the Council at any one time.

68. Irish Constitution, Art. 26 (1), (1) states that "The President may, after consultation with the Council of State, refer any Bill to which this Article applies to the Supreme Court for a decision on the question as to whether such Bill or any specified provision or provisions of such Bill is or are repugnant to this Constitution or to any provision thereof."

69. Irish Constitution, Art. 26.

70. *In re Article* 26 *and the Offences Against the State* (*Amendment*) *Bill*, 1940, 1940 I.R. 470; 74 I.L.T.R. 61. *In re Article* 26 *and the School Attendance Bill*, 1942, 1943 I.R. 334; 77 I.L.T.R. 96. *In re Article* 26 *and the Electoral Amendment Bill*, 1961, 1961 I.R. 169.

71. Irish Constitution, Art. 26 (1), (1).

72. Irish Constitution, Art. 40 (4), (1).
73. *Buckley and Others (Sinn Fein)* v. *The Attorney General and Another,* 1950 I.R. 67.
74. Irish Constitution, Art. 28 (3), (3).
75. *Ibid.*
76. *Richardson and Webster* v. *Athlone Woollen Mills,* 1942 I.R. 581.
77. *O'Donovan* v. *Attorney General,* 1961 I.R. 114; 96 I.L.T.R. 121.
78. *The State (Modern Homes (Ireland) Ltd.)* v. *Dublin Corporation,* 1953 I.R. 202.
79. Local Government (Planning and Development) Act, 1963 repealing Town and Regional Planning Act, 1934 and Town and Regional Planning (Amendment) Act, 1939.
80. For current situation see Solicitors' Act, 1954 as amended by the Solicitors (Amendment) Act, 1960. Apprenticeship and education regulations have been made under this legislation.
81. J. O'Donnell, *How Ireland is Governed,* pp. 86-88.
82. Chief Justice Conor Maguire when he was Attorney General in the 1930s was probably the last to appear personally on behalf of the State.

II

IRISH JUDGES

What is an Irish Judge?

In an attempt to answer this question a study was conducted of the Irish judiciary to determine such background information as birthplace, ethnic background, education, religious commitment, political party affiliation, occupation before appointment, geographic residence at the time of appointment, date of appointment, lawyers in their family relationship, socio-economic status before appointment, paternal occupation, age at time of appointment, and other factors that might in some fashion be influential on the decisions handed down by a judge on the bench and that might indicate in general the type of person a judge is — a composite picture of an Irish judge.

The data were gathered by personal interview of all sitting judges on the Supreme, High, and Circuit courts and of seven of the sitting judges on the District courts. Of the remaining twenty-eight District Court judges (of a total of thirty-five) ten responded to a mailed questionnaire. Thus, seventeen of thirty-five District judges were included in the study. One Supreme Court judge had died and three retired of those appointed under the 1937 Constitution. Two of the retired judges were interviewed personally but information concerning the remaining retired judge and the deceased judge was secured from secondary sources, in the case of the deceased judge, from his son. One retired judge on the High Court was interviewed personally. Thus all of the judges named to the top three courts under the 1937 Constitution are accounted for. In short the study covered nine Supreme Court judges, eight High Court judges, ten Circuit Court judges, and seventeen of thirty-five sitting District Court judges. Thus forty-four judges comprise the group used to develop this profile of an Irish judge.

This is strictly a pioneer study. Nothing of the sort has been done before in Ireland. Its purpose is to determine something not before known with any degree of accuracy — the characteristics of Irish judges, their social and political backgrounds, and something of how they came to be appointed.

Court	Number of sitting judges	Retired	Dead	Personal interview	Questionnaire
Supreme Court	5	3	1	7 (2)*	0
High Court	7	1	0	8	0
Circuit Court	10	0	0	10	0
District Court	35	0	0	7	10
Total	57	4	1	32 (2)*	10

*Information on two judges, one retired and one dead, secured from secondary sources.

The data indicate that it would be well for a person with judicial ambitions to be born in other than a rural setting. Only a little more than a fifth of those named as judges were born in a rural area while almost half were born in a distinctly urban atmosphere, usually Dublin, and the remainder in small towns. Thus the breakdown geographically of birthplaces comes to something less than an equal division between Dublin and the country at large. Being born and reared in Dublin presumably gave the judges-to-be urban advantages including educational opportunities.

When residence at the time of appointment is considered the 'Dublin percentage' goes up. Two-thirds of the judges are Dubliners in this sense. Only one of the sitting or retired Supreme Court judges came from outside the capital, none of the High Court judges and only one of the Circuit Court judges. As might be expected, the bulk of those without Dublin attachments are on the District Court.

Specifically and in practice what is the process of choosing the man who is to be named to a judgeship? A general consensus exists that there are no promises of judgeships for party service and this same consensus holds that no appointments are made of those unqualified for the judicial posts. Statutes require that appointees to the Supreme Court, the High Court and the Circuit Court be practising barristers of at least ten years' standing. Appointees to the District Court must have been practising barristers or solicitors of at least ten years' standing. At the time of this survey, twenty-six of the thirty-five District Court judges were solicitors. These requirements are, of course, always abided by, and one cannot escape the conclusion that only persons that an objective observer would say are qualified otherwise are named. This is not to say that the best person available is always named but that usually those named are of judicial calibre.

However, there is the very realistic point that, with rare exceptions, a person named as judge will be one who is favourably regarded by the Government perhaps out of gratitude for past services either to the party or to the state. Even in the rare instance where an adherent of the opposition party is named this may well be for indirect advantage of the Government party in that such a 'nonpartisan' appointment projects an image of objectivity to the public with concern for the quality of the courts rather than considering only political and partisan factors.

A judicial appointment does not 'just happen'. It is in a very real sense the finest and the most desirable appointment that the Government can make. It is a status appointment. The choice is not made casually. Many persons have a part — perhaps most of them a small part — in the process of selection. The 'inner circles' of the party and of the Government always have in mind potential appointees for judicial vacancies before they actually occur. In the instance of a vacancy on the High Court or the Supreme Court the Attorney General has usually the 'first right of refusal' as it is called. The Attorney General has been named to such a post seven times under the present Constitution. Only Mr Patrick Lynch and Mr Patrick McGilligan were not so appointed. The Attorney General is never appointed to the Circuit or District courts. If he turns down an appointment or if the vacancy is on one of the two lower court levels, informal discussions are held by the Cabinet. The Minister for Justice makes up a list of prospects and presents it in Cabinet meeting. The 'list' may contain a single name. The Ministers may add names to this list. Persons on it may be politically active or politically neutral. Some judges have thought that their work as a counsel in 'state cases' has helped their cause, that this had given them the opportunity to get to know the Taoiseach. Others have had members of the Government as clients and the personal friendship resulting helped. Another judge pointed out that his uncle was a friend of influential persons. One judge said simply that he met the Minister for Justice through a member of parliament and proceeded to tell the Minister that he was interested in an appointment. Persons who feel that they have a chance to be appointed commonly put in an application for the post. No formal vote is taken at the cabinet meeting; an informal agreement on a particular person evolves. If the Taoiseach, the Prime Minister, has a favourite, that man will get the appointment. Certainly no one has ever been named judge over the objections of the Taoiseach. The person chosen is then formally consulted and his consent secured. Then the President, who has not been consulted on the appointment, is told the name of the appointee and the formal appointment is made by the President.

A judgeship is, for what are the pretty obvious reasons of prestige, power and security of tenure among others, a very desirable post, and within the limits of constitutional requirements and good taste there will be discreet influences brought to bear by the aspirant himself or by an *alter ego*. This has involved such a simple thing as a casual suggestion, written or oral. This may well take place long before any actual vacancy occurs and, in any event, is not to be classed as direct 'lobbying' of members of the Cabinet.

As noted above, custom has decreed that in the case of a vacancy on either the High or Supreme Courts the Attorney General is usually to be given the first chance. Actually he may not be tendered the vacancy itself. If it is on the Supreme Court, a member of the High Court may be moved up to that vacancy with the Attorney General then offered the High Court vacancy thus created. The Attorney General's role in this has resulted in some interesting developments. The coalition government of 1948 to 1951 under John Costello named two of its Attorneys General to judgeships. In still another instance an Attorney General whose party was going out of office was named to a judgeship on the last day before the party left office. It is thought that an Attorney General brings to a judicial post a dimension different from that of a normal member of the Bar, since he is regarded as the leader of the Bar.

In some cases prior party political activity or valuable service will have focused attention on a particular individual. In the case of some persons this background activity may go back some time. For example, one judge was named primarily because of his service as a prosecutor during World War II. This was a very dangerous assignment and he had to be given an armed guard. Some of the early judicial appointees under the Constitution had been active in the Dáil Eireann courts (established in 1920 by the revolutionary Dáil, they were abolished in 1922). A number of present-day judges worked for the government as legal advisers or prosecutors. In the 1920s a man appointed to the High Court had been a county judge under the British rule of Ireland. Service to the party or to the government itself by a candidate's father (only about one-third of the fathers had been active) or a wife's family (three judges indicated this sort of activity) has seldom been a factor in appointments but the individual's own service has frequently been a very real factor. About sixteen per cent (15.9%) of the judges in this study had been affiliated with the government in some capacity before appointment and seventy-five per cent had been active in party politics delivering campaign speeches or assisting in other ways. In two instances they had been members of the National Executive, the governing body of the party. One judge said that he had been an early supporter of Fianna Fail back when the party had few supporters at the Bar and his judgeship appointment was a reward. A lower percentage of those named to the Supreme Court had been politically active prior to appointment than those named to other courts, indicating that politics is less of a factor in higher court appointments than in lower.

Very few of the persons named as judges pursued what might be called primarily political careers prior to appointment. As noted, a large number of judicial appointments have been given to politically active or politically aligned persons as a reward for service but this has not been done where the person appointed did not occupy a distinctly favourable professional status. However, partisan political considerations are almost the only influence (in addition to legal qualifications) in the naming of District Court judges. Political considerations become less relevant for the judges of the Circuit Court, the High Court, and the Supreme Court. Political factors are particularly apparent whenever a man from an opposition political party is named to a judgeship. As noted, this is supposed to serve as concrete evidence of the 'nonpartisan' character of judicial appointments. The Fianna Fail party has been in power for all but five of the past thirty-eight years and this situation has resulted in the appointment of younger lawyers than would normally have been expected if there had been periods when the party was out of power with resulting 'backlogs' of judicial candidates. This long period of one-party control has also probably meant that more able lawyers of the opposition parties have been passed over. All judges considered, more than half have been appointed since 1955.

One of the judges interviewed for this study made the statement that almost all judicial appointments are based on partisan political considerations. A former Taoiseach made the statement that 'all things being equal' a person's politics is controlling in such appointments. All Irish governments have to a greater or lesser degree been politically motivated in the making of judicial appointments. The English used judges as patronage and the new government after independence named judges that agreed with its aims. Professor (Senator) John M. Kelly made this point in a speech on the floor of the Senate when he said 'The appointment of judges here has always been a political appointment ever since the British left'[1]. Actually it is surprising that the history of appointments to the Irish bench shows as much agreement as has existed within the Government (and presumably in the legal profession generally) as to the person who should be named. This is not to say that in most appointments the person chosen was the obvious choice of Bar and Government. In fact, some people feel that members of the Bar should be consulted on judicial appointments. Some persons have been named who were temperamentally unsuited for the office and this might have been avoided if members of the legal profession who have an intimate knowledge of the character and personality of the candidate could advise on such appointments.

The very fact that a man has worked his way to his appointment by cultivating political favor is not a very good omen as to his future behavior as a judge. In the result, while Irish judges have generally shown themselves to be fairly independent and immune to pressure from the executive once they are safely installed in office, some of them appear to have proved to be obstructive, overbearing, and arrogant in the way they use their judicial power. It is probable that a good case can be made for the proposition that most members of the Bar could have foreseen such a situation, from their knowledge of the persons concerned, and would not have thought them suitable for judicial appointment. On occasion there is lacking ordinary courtesy in the conduct of proceedings by judges. Most attorneys seem to have had some experience with judges bullying and even insulting witnesses. On one occasion a Circuit Court judge asked a witness who had concluded his testimony what evidence he would have given if he had been on the other side. While it is not always possible to predict how a person will turn out on the bench, if members of the Bar were consulted on appointments the more obvious instances of temperamentally unsuitable persons could be avoided.

It may well be that public opinion is the saving control of the system of political appointment of judges. Another controlling factor is the fact that politicians are well aware that it is bad politics to name a man who is likely to be a bad judge.

Since the statutes require long-term experience in legal work for judicial appointments there is little concern about securing a man of professional competence, and, in spite of what has been said above, there have been laudable efforts to secure men of judicial temperament. At other times 'laudable effort' has not been present. The quality of judges has, on the whole, been high. The Irish courts have not been made a political 'dumping ground' despite the political nature of most appointments. Undoubtedly there are some persons who go into law with the idea of becoming judge as a reward for political service. Kevin O'Higgins once called these people 'legal careerists'. Only about twenty per cent of the judges consulted thought their legal specialty was a factor in their appointment. Many of those interviewed pointed out that true legal specialization is rare in Ireland. As one judge said, 'Almost everybody has a general background'.

Apart from not appointing persons hostile to the Government party, ideology in the sense of liberalism or conservatism seems to have played little part in appointments. 'Extremism' seems to be absent from the Irish bench, and this may well be simply another example of the conscious effort to name capable men, recognizing always the element of practical politics. The persons named are simply not 'extreme'. Only one judge admitted to being definitely far removed from 'center' ideologically. Self-proclaimed liberals are well represented on all court levels. Overall more than forty-three per cent characterize themselves as liberals and only about thirteen per cent admit to conservatism. On the current Supreme Court there appears to be an interesting 3-1-1 division on a 'liberal', 'centrist', 'conservative' basis. Repeatedly, and most sincerely, judges interviewed maintained the 'objectivity' of those on the Irish courts. As one said, once a man 'goes on the bench he abandons entirely all views previously held, feeling himself bound in conscience to empty his mind of all past adherences. He takes an oath on his appointment and, as far as I know, and I have been on the bench for twenty-seven years, no single judge has ever deviated in the slightest way from this high ideal.' Granted that the statement by a judge about the judiciary must be treated with considerable caution, there is still some indication here of an attitude. But subjectivity has reared its head on occasion. There has, for example, been evidence of anti-trade union sentiment on the bench in isolated instances. This simply underlines the point that impartiality is most difficult to obtain in any system. There is always the human element.

Judicial experience apparently has not been a prime consideration in the choice of judges. Very few have been promoted to a higher court, the only real basis for prior judicial experience in the Irish system since there is nothing comparable to the state courts in the United States. Promotion within the Irish judiciary is theoretically possible but offers real difficulties in practice.

By the terms of the Constitution, the District Court judges, who usually are solicitors rather than barristers, cannot become Circuit judges and no barrister has as yet been promoted from the District Court to the Circuit Court. Actually there is only one instance where a judge of the Circuit Court has been promoted to the High Court. Judge Davitt had refused a High Court appointment. Later he was prevailed upon to take a Circuit Court appointment with the understanding that he would be given an appointment to the High Court when a vacancy developed, and this was done. Considering the rather remarkable prestige of Judge Davitt, based in large measure on his part in the establishment of the Republic, this sort of thing is unlikely to happen again. However, promotion from the High Court to the Supreme Court has been almost common. Four of the nine judges who have served on the Supreme Court under the present Constitution were members of the High Court before being named to the Supreme Court. Going back to 1924, only two additional judges had been appointed to the Supreme Court without service on the High Court. No other judges have had any prior judicial experience except as temporary appointees or as a member of a quasi-judicial body, such as labour arbitration commissions, the Censorship of Publications Board, the Mining Commission, the Electoral Revision court, and the Court of Referees.

Two reasons are given for the failure to promote District and Circuit court judges to the High and Supreme Courts. First, the judges of the lower courts generally are considered not to be of the high quality desired for appointees to the upper courts. Second, it is feared that a policy of promoting lower court judges would encourage them to make decisions, in both civil and criminal cases in which the government is a party, favoring the government so as to enhance their chances of promotion.

It should be pointed out in this connection that there is a rather firmly established convention, probably taken over from the English system, that promotion does not take place within the judicial hierarchy except from the High Court to the Supreme Court. A period of service on the High Court is probably the best training ground for a future judge of the Supreme Court. There are certain other recognized avenues of promotion within the system. A District Judge may become President of the District Court which, in effect, gives him the rank and salary of a Circuit Court Judge. Likewise, a Circuit Court Judge may become President of the Circuit Court which will give him the rank and salary of an ordinary judge of the High Court. A judge of the High Court or of the Supreme Court might be named President of the High Court. This would give him not only the rank and salary of a Supreme Court judge but also would place him in judicial status second only to the Chief Justice and should be a strong point in his favor for appointment to Chief Justice if that post should become vacant. Obviously a judge of the High Court or the Supreme Court, on the basis of past practice, is always among those favoured for appointment to the office of Chief Justice.

The non-existence or very limited existence of promotion prospects for the judges is one of the better features of the Irish system, (and the English system) as contrasted with the Continental arrangement of career judges climbing the promotion ladder. This does help to insure that the judge will not be 'looking over his shoulder' toward the Government Buildings whenever he is called on to make some controversial decision.

Another significant factor influencing the appointment of judges is religion. In the matter of religious commitment only about fifteen per cent of all judges are not Roman Catholic. This in a sense reflects the overwhelmingly predominant religious faith of Ireland and reflects also the 'link' with that faith indicated in the Constitution. Actually there are more non-Catholics on the courts than the proportion that their numbers bear to the total population. The Supreme Court at present has one of the five judges not a Catholic, Judge Budd being a member of the Church of Ireland. The religious division on the top court is somewhat analogous to the situation on the Supreme Court of the United States where custom has on occasion dictated that there be one Catholic and one Jew. There is only one member of the Jewish faith on the courts of Ireland, a District Court judge. There are not many Jews in Ireland and these are concentrated in Dublin and Cork. All but one member of the High Court, both sitting and retired, are Catholics. That one judge is a Presbyterian. On the Circuit Court, two of the ten judges are not Catholics, one being a Methodist and one a member of the Church of Ireland. On the District Court three of the thirty-five justices are non-Catholics, one a Baptist, one a member of the Church of Ireland and the third, as noted, a Jew.

On the matter of religion influencing the appointment of judges, as about 95% or more of the population in the Republic of Ireland are Catholics one might well expect that if judicial appointments were made without regard for the question of religion that there might be very few non-Catholics on the bench or possibly none at all over long periods simply on the law of averages. Thus the small number of non-Catholic judges on the bench can well be taken not to reflect any special position given to Catholics but rather the contrary, that is, a conscious effort to give representation to minority interests in an important area where they might be quite unrepresented if no account whatever were taken of religion.

Finally, on the matter of appointments a few items may be added. Members of the Supreme Court are not consulted at all on judicial appointments. Geography is not a factor. There is no attempt to make the judiciary representative and there is no widespread geographical distribution. Some counties have never had a judge appointed from within their boundaries. One judge expressed the possibility that he had been named to get him out of the way politically. Another thought he had been named because a judge was needed on the Western circuit who could speak Irish. The first and only woman judge in Ireland is a District Court judge in Dublin. Her appointment came about as a direct result of a public statement by Sean Lemass when he was Taoiseach that more women should get into civic life. A Supreme Court judge suggested to Miss Kennedy that she should apply, so she wrote to the Minister for Justice and said that she would be interested. Shortly after this she was appointed.

Another judge maintained that his appointment came about because he was an 'outsider' politically, that others being considered were politically involved. By choosing him the party leaders 'got out of a hole' since they were relieved of the difficulty of making a choice from among the politicians.

The salaries of judges are set by statute and thus have been a political issue. This fact motivated the adoption of legislation[2] which gives the Government the power to increase judicial salaries by order in the future. In doing this the draft order will be laid before Dáil Eireann and the Dáil will then have twenty-one days to pass a resolution disapproving of the action. This may have the desired effect of cooling off debate on this subject. The comparatively low salaries of judges restricts the number of persons who are willing to take appointments in spite of prestige and other benefits—this in spite of the unusual statement by at least one judge that the courts are the most expensive governmental activity in Ireland. Actually the country needs and should have a greater number of judges in the interests of speedier and possibly less expensive litigation, at least litigation with fewer delays. The whole complement of judges in all courts runs only to fifty-seven, far below comparable numbers found in France and

Germany as well as the United Kingdom if one includes the Justices of the Peace.

A barrister does not resign from the bar when he goes on the bench, he simply cannot practice during his tenure. The same can be said of a solicitor named to the District Court.

As to age, more judges are appointed when they are between forty and forty-four than at any other age but half of the judges were named when they were past forty-five years of age. No man has been named to the Supreme Court before he was forty.

Most of the judges took degrees from one of the universities but only about half took law degrees. Every barrister as a student does law work at King's Inns. The personal contacts and loyalties thus established cannot be overemphasized in the career pattern of a judge. The amount of sponsorship for judicial office that results can only be conjectured. Further, how much influence for dedicated work there is on the future judges by the intelligent and personally forceful men contacted in this total process is an unknown quantity but by any reasonable calculation it must be considerable. This includes the concepts of leadership, of social values, and of ethical standards that go to make up the whole man become judge.

As to specific institutions, only about one-fourth of the judges went to any university other than University College, Dublin. These went to Trinity College (University of Dublin) with the exception of one who got his degree from University College, Galway. Only three judges who are Catholics received their degrees from Trinity. Two received an LL.B. degree and one did not. No non-Catholics secured their degrees from University College, either at Dublin, Galway or Cork.

None of the Irish judges has been of humble family origin. On the contrary almost two-thirds came from admittedly upper middle class social and economic backgrounds and almost all of the remainder from middle class. A number of the judges attended private preparatory schools such as Castleknock, Belvedere College, Blackrock College, Clongowes Wood, Marbrill College, Haileybury College, and Wesley College, a point emphasizing the middle class background. A goodly number were 'born to the law', that is, more came from families where the father was a lawyer than where the father had any other occupation. Overall more than half of the judges have lawyers somewhere in their family relationship, father, brother, son, wife, or cousin. After law the chief paternal occupation was business on the managerial level, civil service, medicine and farming. While those appointed as judges have themselves been engaged in a variety of occupations removed from the field of law, chiefly teaching, journalism, civil service and business, well over half were in law from the beginning of their productive careers. A few had relatives who had had judicial experience. With this family background the encouragement and finances for the necessary education for law were readily available. Also from such families may well have come the proper attitudes of civic responsibility and social consciousness that produced 'men of the law'.

By far the most of the judges have been and are of Irish ethnic origin. Only about seventeen per cent have not been of pure Irish stock and only one had no Gaelic blood whatsoever. For the most part the non-Irish blood has been English.

What is an Irish judge?

The person who is a judge in Ireland is most likely to have been born in urban surroundings, in fact to have lived in Dublin at the time of appointment, to have had one or more lawyers in his family relationship at least of the degree of kindred of cousin, to have been appointed since 1955, to have graduated from University College, Dublin but without an LL.B. degree, to be from the strata of society known as the upper middle class, to have had no judicial experience prior to appointment, and very definitely he does not feel that his legal specialty (if any) was a factor in his appointment. Further, the typical Irish judge had a father who was a lawyer or in business, he himself is almost certainly a Catholic, he is pure Irish in ancestry, he is almost certainly also to have been a politically active member of the Fianna Fail party at the time of his appointment (although neither his father nor his wife's family was active) and still sympathizes with that party but not quite as enthusiastically as previously, was appointed after he was forty years of age and probably after forty-five. His first self-supporting job was in law as a barrister or a solicitor, he regards himself as a liberal in ideology, and thinks he was named to his judicial post because of his professional status. He believes that the Supreme Court decides cases before it on the basis of the merits of those cases, is convinced of the independence of the judiciary from the executive and legislative branches of the government, and thinks that the relations existing between the courts and the press of the country are very good.

By way of mild comparison, one might note what the results of a poll of justices of the Supreme Court of the United States would be in answer to some of the questions asked of the members of the Irish Supreme Court. Almost two-thirds of those who have served on the United States Supreme Court were from 'political families', that is, those engaged in active partisanship or governmental effort involving real participation. Only about a fourth of the Irish Supreme Court members came from families of this sort. Over one-third of the United States Supreme Court justices have been related by blood or marriage to jurists. The most recent of these is Justice John Marshall Harlan, currently on the Court, a grandson of the earlier Harlan. About 88 per cent of the Irish Supreme Court judges are related to lawyers but only about 22 per cent are related to present or prior judges. Apart from politics, the fathers of American justices were in farming, manufacturing, law, medicine, religion, and education. The Irish judges' fathers were chiefly in law, business, government service, medicine, religion, education, and banking.

Three-fourths of the United States justices were born in urban areas and had remained there for much of their lives. In Ireland 78 per cent of the judges came from an urban background of some sort. It is interesting to note that better than five per cent of the American justices were born outside the United States. One of these was William Paterson of Ireland, named by President Washington. Early Supreme Court members, before the full development of law schools, secured their legal education by serving as law apprentices, but this by no means meant that they had an inferior legal education. Their tutors were frequently among the leaders of the bar. Since the early days all appointees have been law school graduates and about one-third graduates of the prestigious Ivy League schools of law. All Irish judges have had university degrees but only a third have taken the LL.B. degree. All of the American justices over the years have been economically of the middle or upper classes with all that that implies in the way of educational and social advantages. Two-thirds of the Irish judges have come from the upper middle class economically speaking.

In the way of religion the Supreme Court of the United States, like the country itself, has been predominantly Protestant. Various sects have been represented, chiefly the Episcopalian, Presbyterian, Congregational and Unitarian churches. Catholics, Jews, and Quakers have been found less frequently than adherents of other religions. In Ireland about one-fifth of the Supreme Court judges have been Protestant, from the Church of Ireland. As to ethnic background, most American justices have been natives of or descendants of natives of the countries of northwestern Europe. They have been chiefly of English, Welsh, Scotch, and Irish descent. All members of the Irish Supreme Court have been Irish but one judge admitted to some English admixture.

As to occupation before appointment to the Supreme Court, all American justices were engaged in some aspect of the law or of government service. The same has been true of Irish judges. Most in the United States were practising lawyers, some were judges on state courts or lower federal courts and a few in recent times had been law school professors or deans. It is interesting that all Court appointees with possibly one exception (George Shiras) had been active in partisan politics prior to appointment. In Ireland only a little over 55 per cent had been politically active. Political affiliation with the President's party or at least ideological commitment with the President's notions has been uniformly followed in the United States. Basically this has also been true in Ireland.

More than half of those named to the United States Supreme Court had some prior judicial experience. About one-half of the Irish Supreme Court had prior judicial experience, all of it on the High Court.

Interview Schedule

Birthplace (urban, small town, rural)
Geographic residence at time of appointment
Occupation before appointment (chief clients?)
Lawyers in family relationship
Date of appointment
Education (including private or public elementary and secondary schools)
Socio-economic status before appointment
Prior judicial experience
Legal specialty a factor in appointment
Paternal occupation
Religious commitment
Ethnic background
Political party affiliation at time of appointment
Affiliation today
Age at time of appointment
First self-supporting job
Was father politically active? Wife's family active?
Political activity prior to appointment
Ideological viewpoint
Influences on appointment (professional status, Presidential advisers, Department of Justice, the Bar, Members of Parliament, Members of Cabinet, reward for service, influential persons, other reasons)

Since admittedly court decisions are not arrived at completely
apart from other influences, in your opinion what specific factors
have had an effect on court decisions in your experience?
Relations of courts with executive and legislative branches
Reversals of decisions by legislation
Compliance with decisions
Relations of courts with the press including law reviews.

REFERENCES

1. *Parliamentary Debates, Seanad Eireann,* Wednesday, December 16, 1970,
   p. 162.
2. Courts (Supplemental Provisions) (Amendment) (No. 2) Act, 1968 (No. 21
   of 1968), Sec. 1.

Summary Table

	Supreme		High		Circuit (10)	District (17)	Totals (44)
	(5) Sitting	(4) Former	(7) Sitting	(1) Former			
Birthplace:							
Dublin	2(40%)	2(50%)	2(28.5%)	1(100%)	4(40%)	4(23.5%)	15(34.0%)
Other urban	1(20%)	0	2(28.5%)	0	2(20%)	1(5.8%)	6(13.6%)
Small town	2(40%)	0	2(28.5%)	0	2(20%)	8(47%)	14(31.8%)
Rural	0	2(50%)	1(14.2%)	0	2(20%)	4(23.5%)	9(20.4%)
Residence at time of appointment:							
Dublin	4(80%)	4(100%)	7(100%)	1(100%)	9(90%)	5(29.4%)	30(68.1%)
Cork	0	0	0	0	1(10%)	1(5.8%)	2(4.5%)
Small town	1(20%)	0	0	0	0	7(41.1%)	8(18.1%)
Rural	0	0	0	0	0	4(23.5%)	4(9.0%)
Occupation before appointment:							
Barrister	4(80%)	2(50%)	4(57.1%)	1(100%)	10(100%)	5(29.4%)	26(59.0%)
Solicitor	0	0	0	0	0	11(64.7%)	11(25.1%)
Attorney General	1(20%)	2(50%)	3(42.8%)	0	0	0	6(13.6%)
Civil Servant	0	0	0	0	0	1(5.8%)	1(2.2%)
Lawyers in family:							
Yes	4(80%)	4(100%)	4(57.1%)	0	4(40%)	7(41.1%)	23(52.2%)
No	1(20%)	0	3(42.8%)	1(100%)	6(60%)	10(5.8%)	21(47.7%)
Date of original appointment:							
Before 1936	0	1(25%)	0	1(100%)	0	0	2(4.5%)
1936–1939	0	1(25%)	0	0	0	0	1(2.2%)
1940–1944	0	1(25%)	0	0	1(10%)	2(11.7%)	4(9.0%)
1945–1949	0	1(25%)	0	0	1(10%)	4(23.5%)	6(13.6%)
1950–1954	2(40%)	0	3(42.8%)	0	1(10%)	2(11.7%)	8(18.1%)
1955–1959	0	0	0	0	4(40%)	1(5.8%)	6(13.6%)
1960–1964	1(20%)	0	2(28.5%)	0	2(20%)	3(17.6%)	7(15.9%)
1965–1969	2(40%)	0	2(28.5%)	0	1(10%)	5(29.4%)	10(22.7%)

Summary Table—continued

	Supreme Sitting	Supreme Former	High Sitting	High Former	Circuit	District	Totals
Education:							
UCD	4(80%)	2(50%)	0	0	3(30%)	6(35.2%)	15(34.0%)
UCD, LL.B.	0	1(25%)	5(71.4%)	1(100%)	4(40%)	2(11.7%)	13(29.5%)
UCD, Trinity	0	0	0	0	1(10%)	0	1(2.2%)
Trinity	0	1(25%)	2(28.5%)	0	2(20%)	3(17.6%)	6(13.6%)
Trinity, LL.B.	1(20%)	0	0	0	0	1(5.8%)	4(9.0%)
UCG, LL.B.	0	0	0	0	0	1(5.8%)	1(2.2%)
No answer	0	0	0	0	0	4(23.5%)	4(9.0%)
Socio-economic status before appointment:							
Upper middle class	5(100%)	1(25%)	6(85.7%)	0	7(70%)	7(41.1%)	26(59.0%)
Middle class	0	2(50%)	1(14.2%)	1(100%)	2(20%)	5(29.4%)	11(25.1%)
Lower middle class	0	0	0	0	1(10%)	0	1(2.2%)
No answer	0	1(25%)	0	0	0	5(29.4%)	6(13.6%)
Prior judicial experience:							
High Court	2(40%)	4(100%)	0	0	0	0	6(13.6%)
Temporary appointment	0	0	0	0	3(30%)	1(5.8%)	4(9.0%)
Quasi-Judicial body	0	0	0	0	0	1(5.8%)	1(2.2%)
Legal speciality a factor in appointment:							
Yes	2(40%)	0	1(14.2%)	0	0	5(29.4%)	8(18.1%)
No	3(60%)	3(75%)	5(71.4%)	1(100%)	9(90%)	9(52.9%)	30(68.1%)
No answer	0	1(25%)	1(14.2%)	0	1(10%)	3(17.6%)	6(13.6%)
Paternal occupation:							
Law	2(40%)	1(25%)	2(28.5%)	0	2(20%)	5(29.4%)	12(27.2%)
Business	1(20%)	0	1(14.2%)	0	4(40%)	3(17.6%)	9(20.4%)
Civil Servant	1(20%)	0	0	0	1(10%)	3(17.6%)	5(11.3%)
Farming	0	0	0	0	1(10%)	2(11.7%)	3(6.8%)
Medicine	0	1(25%)	1(14.2%)	0	1(10%)	0	3(6.8%)
Teaching	0	1(25%)	0	0	0	1(5.8%)	2(4.5%)
Engineering	0	0	1(14.2%)	0	1(10%)	0	2(4.5%)
Clergy	0	1(25%)	1(14.2%)	0	0	0	2(4.5%)
Industry	0	0	0	0	0	1(5.8%)	1(2.2%)
Banking	1(20%)	0	0	0	0	0	1(2.2%)
Chemist (Druggist)	0	0	0	0	0	1(5.8%)	1(2.2%)
Independently wealthy	0	0	0	0	0	1(5.8%)	1(2.2%)
Journalism	0	0	1(14.2%)	1(100%)	0	0	2(4.5%)

Summary Table—continued

	Supreme		High		Circuit	District	Totals
	Sitting	Former	Sitting	Former			
Religious commitment:							
Roman Catholic	4(80%)	3(75%)	6(85.7%)	1(100%)	8(80%)	15(88.2%)	37(84.0%)
Church of Ireland	1(20%)	1(25%)	0	0	1(10%)	1(5.8%)	4(9.0%)
Presbyterian	0	0	1(14.2%)	0	0	0	1(2.2%)
Methodist	0	0	0	0	1(10%)	0	1(2.2%)
Jewish	0	0	0	0	0	1(5.8%)	1(2.2%)
Ethnic background:							
Irish	4(80%)	3(75%)	6(85.7%)	1(100%)	9(90%)	14(82.3%)	37(84.0%)
Irish-English	1(20%)	0	1(14.2%)	0	0	0	2(4.5%)
French, Irish, English	0	0	0	0	1(10%)	0	1(2.2%)
English, Russian, Polish	0	0	0	0	0	1(5.8%)	1(2.2%)
No answer	0	1(25%)	0	0	0	2(11.7%)	3(6.8%)
Party affiliation at appointment:							
Fianna Fail	3(60%)	2(50%)	6(85.7%)	0	7(70%)	14(82.3%)	32(72.7%)
Fine Gael	1(20%)	1(25%)	0	1(100%)	1(10%)	0	4(9.0%)
None	1(20%)	0	1(14.2%)	0	0	2(11.7%)	4(9.0%)
Labour	0	0	0	0	1(10%)	1(5.8%)	2(4.5%)
Republican (Interparty)	0	0	0	0	1(10%)	0	1(2.2%)
No answer	0	1(25%)	0	0	0	0	1(2.2%)
Party sympathy now:							
Fianna Fail	3(60%)	1(25%)	4(57.1%)	0	3(30%)	11(64.7%)	22(50.0%)
Fine Gael	1(20%)	0	0	1(100%)	0	0	2(4.5%)
Labour	0	0	0	0	1(10%)	1(5.8%)	2(4.5%)
None	1(20%)	2(50%)	3(42.8%)	0	6(60%)	5(29.4%)	17(38.6%)
No answer	0	1(25%)	0	0	0	0	1(2.2%)

Summary Table—continued

	Supreme		High		Circuit	District	Totals
	Sitting	Former	Sitting	Former			
Age at first appointment :							
30 to 34	0	0	0	1(100%)	0	2(11.7%)	3(6.8%)
35 to 39	0	0	0	0	2(20%)	3(17.6%)	5(11.3%)
40 to 44	2(40%)	2(50%)	3(42.8%)	0	5(50%)	2(11.7%)	14(31.8%)
45 to 49	1(20%)	1(25%)	1(14.2%)	0	1(10%)	2(11.7%)	6(13.6%)
50 to 54	1(20%)	0	2(28.5%)	0	1(10%)	6(35.2%)	10(22.7%)
55 to 59	0	1(25%)	0	0	1(10%)	1(5.8%)	3(6.8%)
60 to 64	1(20%)	0	1(14.2%)	0	0	1(5.8%)	2(4.5%)
65 to 70	0	0	0	0	0	0	1(2.2%)
First self-supporting job :							
Barrister	3(60%)	1(25%)	4(57.1%)	1(100%)	5(50%)	2(11.7%)	16(36.3%)
Solicitor	0	1(25%)	1(14.2%)	0	3(30%)	8(47%)	10(22.7%)
Teacher	1(20%)	0	1(14.2%)	0	1(10%)	2(11.7%)	7(15.9%)
Business	0	0	0	0	0	1(5.8%)	2(4.5%)
Civil servant	0	0	1(14.2%)	0	0	1(5.8%)	2(4.5%)
Journalist	1(20%)	1(25%)	0	0	0	0	1(2.2%)
Acting	0	0	0	0	1(10%)	1(5.8%)	1(2.2%)
Army	0	0	0	0	0	0	1(2.2%)
Law office work	0	0	0	0	0	1(5.8%)	1(2.2%)
Nursing	0	0	0	0	0	1(5.8%)	1(2.2%)
No answer	0	1(25%)	0	0	0	1(5.8%)	1(2.2%)
Political activity prior to appointment :							
Yes	4(80%)	2(50%)	5(71.4%)	0	9(90%)	14(82.3%)	34(77.2%)
No	1(20%)	2(50%)	2(28.5%)	1(100%)	1(10%)	3(17.6%)	10(22.7%)
Father politically active :							
Yes	0	2(50%)	2(28.5%)	1(100%)	5(50%)	8(47%)	18(40.9%)
No	5(100%)	2(50%)	5(71.4%)	0	5(50%)	9(52.9%)	26(59%)

Note: Only three judges, all on the two lower court levels, said their wives' families had been politically active.

Summary Table—continued

	Supreme		High		Circuit	District	Totals
	Sitting	Former	Sitting	Former			
Ideological viewpoint:							
Liberal	3(60%)	1(25%)	2(28.5%)	1(100%)	6(60%)	6(35.2%)	19(43.1%)
Centre	1(20%)	1(25%)	2(28.5%)	0	2(20%)	4(23.5%)	10(22.7%)
Right of centre	1(20%)	1(25%)	2(28.5%)	0	1(10%)	1(5.8%)	6(13.6%)
No answer	0	1(25%)	1(14.2%)	0	1(10%)	6(35.2%)	9(20.4%)
Factors influencing appointment:*							
Professional status	3(60%)	1(25%)	3(42.8%)	0	5(50%)	11(64.7%)	23(52.2%)
Reward for service	0	0	2(28.5%)	1(100%)	1(10%)	2(11.7%)	6(13.6%)
Attorney General post	1(20%)	2(50%)	2(28.5%)	0	0	0	5(11.3%)
Influential persons	0	0	0	0	3(30%)	1(5.8%)	4(9.0%)
Department of Justice	0	0	0	0	0	1(5.8%)	1(2.2%)
Knowledge of Irish Language	0	0	0	0	1(10%)	0	1(2.2%)
No answer	1(20%)	1(25%)	0	0	0	2(11.7%)	4(9.0%)

*It should be noted that this is a subjective assessment by the judges themselves of the basis on which they were appointed.

III

IRISH LAW

The law of Ireland in the broad sense of the term embodies four elements—constitutional law, statutory law, common law, and administrative law. The Constitution of 1937 is the basic law of the state. Any statute enacted by the Oireachtas, the parliament of Ireland, to be valid must not be repugnant to the Constitution. Since Ireland is a unitary type of government the central government is deemed to possess all governmental powers not prohibited to it by the terms of the Constitution so there is not the need to look for some legal basis in the Constitution for action, a constitutional 'peg' on which to hang the action—as there is in the United States. As already noted, only the High Court or the Supreme Court has jurisdiction to determine the validity of a statute under the Constitution[1]. The decisions of these courts and particularly the Supreme Court's decisions constitute the bulk of Irish 'constitutional law'.

Statutory law in Ireland is a bit more complex. Four different groups of statutes are involved. First, there are the statutes of the Parliament of Ireland, sometimes called the Old Irish Parliament. This body began in 1310 and ended with the Act of Union in 1800. A number of these enactments are still valid but a fair number are now no longer applicable. Some have been specifically repealed. These 1310 to 1800 statutes are referred to as 'Acts of the Parliament of Ireland'. Secondly, there are the statutes applied to Ireland by Poyning's Law in 1495. Under this statute passed by the Irish Parliament all English statutes concerned with the common good were to be applied to Ireland. These comprise fifteen statutes enacted by the British Parliament from 1226 to 1429, some of which are still in force. Thus for this period, and until the establishment of Grattan's Parliament in 1782, the Irish Parliament was a subordinate legislative body. This was asserted in statutory form by an enactment which stated that "the kingdom of Ireland has been, is and of right ought to be subordinate unto and dependent upon the imperial crown of Great Britain as being inseparably united and annexed thereunto, and that the King's Majesty, by and with the advice and consent of the Lords Spiritual and Temporal and Commons of Great Britain in Parliament assembled, had, hath, and of right ought to have full power and authority to make laws and statutes of sufficient force and validity to bind the people and kingdom of Ireland"[2]. Thirdly, for the period between 1800 and 1922, there are the statutes enacted in London by the parliament of the 'United Kingdom of Great Britain and Ireland'. Some of these applied to both England and Ireland but others applied only to Ireland. These are known as 'Acts of the Parliament of the late United Kingdom of Great Britain and Ireland'. The Irish Free State Constitution of 1922 provided that the laws in force "at the date of the coming into operation of this Constitution, shall continue to be of full force and effect until the same or any of them shall have been repealed or amended by enactment of the Oireachtas . . ."[3] The Constitution of 1937 makes a similar provision with the limitation "subject to this Constitution and to the extent to which they are not inconsistent therewith"[4]. There was a similar limitation in the Irish Free State Constitution[5]. The fourth group of statutes are the Acts passed by the Oireachtas since 1922. Those enacted between 1922 and 1937 are known as 'Acts of the Oireachtas of Saorstat Eireann' and those enacted since 1937 are called 'Acts of the Oireachtas'.

The common law of Ireland, like that of the United States, came from England. At the beginning of the 17th century English common law had supplanted the *brehon* laws, the system of laws prevailing in Ireland from the earliest times. These had been committed to writing before the middle of the eighth century and constituted one of the most ancient legal systems of Western Europe. This was 'jurist-made law' based on immemorial usage. The common law of England is found in the reported decisions of the Royal Courts and this was imported into Ireland. In England, reports of decisions of the courts were written by lawyers and published from time to time. About the end of the 18th century these began to be published regularly. Since the middle of the 19th century this series has been called *The Law Reports,* a product of private enterprise, not a government publication. A similar situation developed in Ireland with *The Irish Reports.* The concept of and the rules of equity invoked in England to supplement the common law also were adopted in Ireland. Both common law and equity involved application of the doctrine of binding precedent or *stare decisis.* However, both statutory law and common law must conform with the basic law, the Constitution.

The fourth element in the law of Ireland is administrative law. This term applies not only to that portion of statutory and common law dealing primarily with the relations of government with citizens but also to the orders or ordinances issued by executive officials or bodies. In the complexities of modern society this branch of the law has assumed great importance not only in Ireland but almost everywhere.

In the realm of Irish constitutional law one aspect is of particular interest, civil liberties. Because Ireland is a unitary state there is no need to consider substantive powers of the government since all legal power is vested in the government except when constitutional limitations restrict those powers. Such limitations involve primarily what are called civil liberties, in any legal context a 'fashionable' topic in 'the afternoon of the twentieth century'. In the United States in the past quarter of a century this has at times seemed to be almost the sole concern of the Supreme Court, and it is interesting to note the comparative Irish scene both as to the constitutional provisions regarding rights and liberties and the interpretations of these by the Supreme Courts of the two countries. Too, it seems proper to consider civil liberties in connection with a study of the judiciary because of their very close connection with court operations.

In both the Constitution of the United States and the Constitution of Ireland there are guarantees of rights. In the Irish Constitution Articles 40 to 44 inclusive contain these fundamental rights and limitations on government while the guarantees in the United States Constitution are primarily in the Bill of Rights, Amendments I to IX inclusive, as well as in Article I, Sections 9 and 10 of the original Constitution and the Fourteenth Amendment. The federal system of the United States makes it necessary to include restrictions on both the federal and state governments. Ireland's unitary scheme has no such problem.

In any discussion such as this it should be borne in mind that limitations in the Irish Constitution are very definitely more casually regarded than are similar provisions in the Constitution of the United States. Too, in the Irish Constitution the guarantees are to 'citizens' rather than to 'persons' as in the United States Constitution but this has generally been regarded as not excluding aliens from the benefits of the guarantees. However the Irish Supreme Court in *Nicolau's Case*[6] expressly reserved for another case and time the answer to that question. The guarantee of habeas corpus in the Constitution appears to be to 'persons' rather than to 'citizens'[7].

Article 40, Section 1. All citizens shall, as human persons, be held equal before the law.

This shall not be held to mean that the State shall not in its enactments have due regard to differences of capacity, physical and moral, and of social function.

There have been few Supreme Court applications of this provision, most notably in the *Nicolau's Case* of 1966 in which the Court held that it was not a denial of the guaranteed equality to treat the natural father of an illegitimate child different from the treatment accorded the natural mother in an adoption case involving the child[8]. The Court has stated that this provision is not to be held "in respect of any particular citizen, or class of citizens, but extends to all the citizens of the State" and the determination of the extent of the guarantee is "a matter peculiarly within the province of the Oireachtas and any attempt by this Court to control the Oireachtas in the exercise of this function would in our opinion be a usurpation of its authority"[9].

Article 40, Section 2, Sub-section 1. Titles of nobility shall not be conferred by the State.

Sub-section 2. No title of nobility or of honour may be accepted by any citizen except with the prior approval of the Government.

There has been no Supreme Court case interpreting or applying this provision, but it is regularly ignored especially in regard to hereditary peerages and Papal honours.

Article 40, Section 3, Sub-section 1. The State guarantees in its laws to respect, and, as far as practicable, by its laws to defend and vindicate the personal rights of the citizen.

Sub-section 2. The State shall, in particular, by its laws protect as best it may from unjust attack and, in the case of injustice done, vindicate the life, person, good name, and property rights of every citizen.

The Irish courts have generally held that the acts of administrative authorities can be voided by a court only if they are *ultra vires* or contrary to 'natural justice'. In *Brendan Dunne, Ltd.* v. *Fitzpatrick and Others*[10] the Court granted an injunction against picketing and this provision of the Constitution was held to confer a right on both employers and workers to use their property and labour without interference unless such interference was made legitimate by law.

At this point in time the 'personal rights' guaranteed by this part of the Constitution are as yet largely undefined but probably include the "right to have recourse to the High Court to defend and vindicate a legal right"[11]. Further consideration was given to this provision in *Ryan* v. *Attorney General*[12] and the Court impliedly held that bodily integrity, here the Health (Fluoridation of Water Supplies) Act, 1960 was upheld, is included in the guarantee along with, apparently, an undefined residue of personal rights over and above those guarantees specifically enumerated in the Constitution. Earlier the Court had held that placing physical restraint on mentally infirm persons was not an infringement of 'personal rights[13]. Overall the Court has allowed the Oireachtas a rather free hand in this matter.

 Article 40, Section 4, Sub-section 1. No citizen shall be deprived of his personal liberty save in accordance with law.

The phrase 'save in accordance with law' has been interpreted generally as meaning 'ordinary legislation'. The outstanding exception is *Burke's Case*[14] which was later effectively overruled by the reenactment of the legislation in question and its reference to the Supreme Court by the President. Under Article 34, Section 3, Sub-section 3 this makes the legislation proof against constitutional challenge. Pertinent here is the decision by the Court in *The State (Browne)* v. *Feran and Others*,[15] which overruled *Burke's Case* in that the Court refused to apply that part of *Burke* that no appeal lay against the grant of an order of habeas corpus in favour of a person in custody.

 Article 40, Section 4, Sub-section 2. Upon complaint being made by or on behalf of any person to the High Court or any judge thereof alleging that such person is being unlawfully detained, the High Court and any and every judge thereof to whom such complaint is made shall forthwith enquire into the said complaint and may order the person in whose custody such person is detained to produce the body of such person before the High Court on a named day and to certify in writing the grounds of his detention, and the High Court shall, upon the body of such person being produced before that Court and after giving the person in whose custody he is detained an opportunity of justifying the detention, order the release of such person from such detention unless satisfied that he is being detained in accordance with the law.

 Sub-section 3. Where the body of a person alleged to be unlawfully detained is produced before the High Court in pursuance of an order in that behalf made under this section and that Court is satisfied that such person is being detained in accordance with a law but that such law is invalid having regard to the provisions of this Constitution, the High Court

shall refer the question of the validity of such law to the
Supreme Court by way of case stated and may, at the time
of such reference or at any time thereafter, allow the said
person to be at liberty on such bail and subject to such
conditions as the High Court shall fix until the Supreme Court
has determined the question so referred to it.

Sub-section 4. The High Court before which the body of a
person alleged to be unlawfully detained is to be produced in
pursuance of an order in that behalf made under this section
shall, if the President of the High Court or, if he is not
available, the senior judge of that Court who is available so
directs in respect of any particular case, consist of three
judges and shall, in every other case, consist of one judge only.

Sub-section 5. Where an order is made under this section by
the High Court or a judge thereof for the production of the
body of a person who is under sentence of death, the High
Court or such judge thereof shall further order that the
execution of the said sentence of death shall be deferred until
after the body of such person has been produced before the
High Court and the lawfulness of his detention has been
determined and if, after such deferment, the detention of such
person is determined to be lawful, the High Court shall
appoint a day for the execution of the said sentence of death
and that sentence shall have effect with the substitution of the
day so appointed for the day originally fixed for the execution
thereof.

Sub-section 6. Nothing in this section, however, shall be
invoked to prohibit, control, or interfere with any act of the
Defence Forces during the existence of a state of war or
armed rebellion.

Habeas corpus procedure is thus detailed in Article 40, Section
4 and Sub-sections. It is clear that once the High Court has
determined that a prisoner's detention is lawful no further
application to another judge of the High Court on that question can
be had. However, appeal may then be taken to the Supreme Court
under Article 34, Section 4, Sub-section 4 since there has been no
legislative exception to such appeals[16].

Article 40, Section 5. The dwelling of every citizen is
inviolable and shall not be forcibly entered save in accordance
with law.

This provision has apparently been considered by the Courts
only once. In a case of search and seizure in which the police
(Gardaí) had searched a house different from the one named in the
warrant. In *The People (Attorney General)* v. *O'Brien*[17] the

Supreme Court refused to hold the evidence thus secured inadmissible at the trial. The opinion by Judge Walsh noted that since there was not "a deliberate and conscious violation of the accused's constitutional rights", that is, the evidence was obtained in ignorance of the defect in the warrant, the evidence could not be excluded.

There is in the Irish Constitution no provision comparable to the Fourth Amendment of the Constitution of the United States that 'The right of the people to be secure in their persons, houses, papers, and effects, against unreasonable searches and seizures, shall not be violated, and no warrants shall issue, but upon probable cause, supported by oath or affirmation, and particularly describing the place to be searched, and the persons or things to be seized.' In Ireland an arrested person might base a complaint on Article 43, Section 4, Sub-section 1, as noted, or he might claim violation of a statute or of common law. A warrant may be issued on a complaint filed by an officer before a judge or a Peace Commissioner. If the complaint is of a serious nature there must be an oath by the informant and the whole must be reduced to writing. Then the arrested person is to be informed of the charge and taken 'as soon as is reasonably practicable' before the proper judicial officer. Under present statutes the police are rather free to arrest and interrogate persons[18]. Under one statute they may enter a person's home or business premises without consent of the person whenever the officers have grounds for suspicion that an offense is being or has been, committed. In this case it would appear that not even a reasonable suspicion is needed for entry.[19]

The phrase 'in accordance with law' is used in several articles of the Constitution and the Court has noted that 'we are of the opinion that it means in accordance with law as it exists at the time when the particular Article is invoked and sought to be applied. In this Article [40, 41] it means the law as it exists at the time when the legality of the detention arises for determination'[20]. Such an interpretation appears to make useless many so-called constitutional guarantees.

There is no provision for indictment in the Irish Constitution as in the Fifth Amendment of the United States Constitution that 'No person shall be held to answer for a capital, or otherwise infamous crime, unless on a presentment or indictment of a grand jury, except in cases arising in the land or naval forces, or in the militia, when in actual service in time of war or public danger.' In Ireland the person suspected of having committed an 'indictable offense' is brought before a District Judge. The judge decides whether the accused is to be tried summarily, a minor offence, or not. If not, either because the justice does not have the authority to hear the case or the defence objects to a summary trial, there is then a preliminary hearing by the justice. The accused can be present with counsel and there can be cross-examination. Then the justice decides whether to send the accused for trial or not, and this may be for an offence other than the one charged. Also the justice may decide whether to admit the defendant to bail or not. When the accused has been sent for trial before a judge and jury in the Circuit Court or the Central Criminal Court an 'indictment' is prepared by the prosecution and the whole is hedged about with few procedural requirements. It may be in non-precise terms, it may be amended and need not state all of the essential elements of the crime. It is possible that the accused may not really have firm knowledge of the real basis of the charge against him, but if this is shown, the court will either quash the indictment or adjourn the case to enable the accused to consider his position.

The technical rules have been relaxed in recent years but it is not intended that the accused may not have firm knowledge of the real basis of the charge against him. The Criminal Justice (Administration) Act, 1924, Section 4 requires that 'Every indictment shall contain and shall be sufficient if it contains a statement of the specific offence or offences with which the accused is charged, together with such particulars as may be necessary for giving reasonable information as to the nature of the charge'[21].

The preliminary hearing, therefore, is the procedural step at which it is decided whether the accused should be held for trial or not. This decision involves much discretion on the part of the prosecution but particularly does it involve discretion on the part of the justice. The seriousness of an offense is determined by the Supreme Court on the basis of the punishment prescribed (this being the most important factor), the moral guilt, the state of the law when the constitution was adopted, and public opinion at the time[22].

There is no provision in the Irish Constitution like that of the Sixth Amendment of the United States Constitution that "In all criminal prosecutions, the accused shall . . . be informed of the nature and the cause of the accusation . . ." Ireland is a signatory of the Convention of Human Rights and Fundamental Freedoms which in Article 6 (3) (a) does contain the guarantee that an accused person is to be informed promptly of the charge against him. He would, of course, have similar rights under the common law[23]. Under present Irish statutes there are two great dangers to the carrying out of this provision. (1) Legislation at times is

vague resulting in uncertainty as to just what action is criminal.
(2) A person may be arrested and detained indefinitely after a
Government proclamation that the public safety will thereby be
more secure[24]. Article 6 of the Convention also provides that the
accused is to be informed of the charge 'in a language which he
understands.' In a case that went to the Supreme Court[25] the
defendant, who understood no Irish, had been accused of violation
of the Road Traffic Act, 1933, namely driving in a manner and at
a speed dangerous to the public. Summonses and court proceedings
were in English but notices of intention to prosecute were in
Irish. The Garda who served the notices explained the contents in
English and the Court held this explanation to be adequate. Under
Article 8, Section 2, Sub-section 3 of the Constitution either Irish
or English can be used for official purposes.

Proceeding further with the matter of guarantees surrounding
criminal prosecution it should be noted that there is no require-
ment either in the Irish or the United States constitutions that
an accused person must be admitted to bail. In the Irish Constitution there is not, as there is in the American, prohibition of
excessive bail[26]. The courts over the years have adhered to English
doctrine that excessive bail shall not be required, but the matter
is subject to judicial discretion[27]. Convicted persons are obviously
in a different position in regard to bail in Ireland and the United
States[28]. Claims of excessive bail in a lower court may be appealed.

There is no guarantee in the Irish Constitution comparable to
that of the Sixth Amendment in the United States Constitution
that in all criminal prosecutions the accused shall have the assistance of counsel for his defense. The provision for counsel in the
Convention for the Protection of Human Rights and Fundamental
Freedoms[29] cannot be relied on before an Irish court because this
has not been specifically accepted by the Oireachtas except in the
very narrow sense that right to counsel is recognized in current
law[30]. Such aid has been on a voluntary basis on the part of the
Irish lawyers, and the records show that in a majority of the cases
in which convictions were had the accused did not have counsel.
Beginning in 1961 efforts were made to secure free legal aid in
limited types of cases, that is, those of sufficient gravity to justify
counsel and state-assisted legal aid is now available for defendants
in poor financial circumstances involved in serious criminal
charges[31]. Moreover, by special arrangement between the Supreme
Court, the Attorney General, and the Minister for Finance there
is in operation a system for assigning counsel to poor plaintiffs
in habeas corpus and other important state side applications when
the High Court or the Supreme Court certifies that the litigant

should have the assistance of counsel. The Supreme Court's decision in *Tynan and Woods* has been credited with bringing about this arrangement[32].

In both Ireland and the United States defendants in criminal cases are guaranteed trial by jury[33]. In Ireland minor offenses are specifically exempt from jury trial and in both countries a jury trial may be waived by the accused[34]. In both countries the right to a jury trial does not extend to cases of criminal contempt or to trials by military tribunals. The number of jurors is twelve but may be reduced to ten in Ireland without the consent of the accused in case of the death or incapacity of a juror or jurors. However, the judge may stop the trial even if only one juror dies or becomes incapacitated. A judge also may discharge a juror because of the death or serious illness of a near relation. The jury, however, may never be reduced below ten members[35]. The details of the Irish jury system differ from those of the United States system. For instance, there is not the same care exercised in Ireland in insuring the presence of an impartial jury. Also in Ireland certain courts are exempt from the guarantee of a jury trial when the Government is satisfied that ordinary courts are inadequate to secure effective administration of justice and preservation of peace and order[36].

The provision of the Irish Constitution guaranteeing a public trial[37] is less positive than that in the Sixth Amendment of the United States Constitution. Under the Irish Constitution exceptions may be made by statute, and specifically excluded by the terms of the Constitution[38] are persons coming before a special criminal court or a military tribunal[39]. Laws have been passed excluding certain criminal proceedings from the guarantee of a public trial.[40]

Once again, this time in regard to witnesses at a trial, the Irish Constitution contains no provision comparable to that in the Sixth Amendment of the United States Constitution that in all criminal prosecutions the accused shall have the right "to be confronted with the witnesses against him; to have compulsory process for obtaining witnesses in his favor . . . '

Irish statutes permit the use of depositions taken at the time of the preliminary investigation with certain limitations[41]. Specifically these are that the deponent be dead or so ill as not to be able to attend the trial and that the deposition was taken in the presence of the accused and the accused or his counsel had the opportunity of cross-examining the deponent. Except in case of death the consent of the accused is needed to admit depositions taken at the request of the prosecution. Thus the use of the deposition is more restricted than in the United States.

In Ireland in practice there have been occasions when the right of confrontation has been denied[42]. Also under Irish law a defendant must be given a list of witnesses that are to be used against him and he has the right to be present at the preliminary hearing[43].

The rather famous Fifth Amendment guarantee of the United States Constitution that 'No person . . . shall be compelled in any criminal case to be a witness against himself . . .' has no counterpart in the Irish Constitution. The right is protected by statute[44] but the protection thus afforded is not as great as that in the United States Constitution. For example, a trial judge in Ireland may comment on the failure of a defendant to testify. As recently interpreted by the Supreme Court of the United States[45], this is not possible under the Fifth Amendment. Also the Irish situation offers the usual danger of any arrangement based on a statute in that the guarantees can be set aside by a subsequent statute[46].

The words 'due process of law' are not used in the Irish Constitution. The courts could have interpreted 'due course of law' and 'save in accordance with law' and other expressions[47] as equivalent to due process as interpreted in the United States but they have not done so. These clauses in the Constitution have not been interpreted as adding anything to individual rights.

The Supreme Court has adopted as a guiding principle the presumption of constitutionality of any statute enacted under the present Irish Constitution. The burden of proof, and a heavy burden, is on the party who challenges the validity of such a statute[48]. In a sense this is a reaffirmation of parliamentary supremacy. Apparently any act passed by the Oireachtas will be upheld unless clearly contrary to a constitutional provision regardless of how the statute affects personal rights[49].

As for a guarantee against an accused being placed in jeopardy twice for the same offense, there is no constitutional provision in Ireland on this. In the United States a provision of the Fifth Amendment protects against this. However, under Irish statutory law the matter of double jeopardy is covered to a considerable extent and the common law principle of *autrefois acquit* also applies. Since this protection is not guaranteed by the Constitution it is, of course, always subject to legislative change[50].

There is nothing in the Irish Constitution on cruel and unusual punishments comparable to the Eighth Amendment provision of the United States Constitution. In a peripheral matter, the Supreme Court of Ireland in a case involving a sentence that was alleged to be for more than the 'usual' term for the offence, (two years) implied that there would be judicial interference with 'cruel and unusual' sentences if an appeal would be sought in time in the orthodox manner[51].

Continuing with the comparative analysis of the Irish and United States Constitutions in the area of criminal prosecution, the ex post facto guarantees of the United States document in Article One, Sections Nine and Ten are mirrored in the Irish Constitution in Article 15, Section 5 which states that 'The Oireachtas shall not declare acts to be infringements of the law which were not so at the date of their commission'. This falls somewhat short of the interpretation given in the United States guarantee[52] inasmuch as there is nothing to guard against increased punishment, the aggravation of a crime, or changes in the rules of evidence. The Emergency Powers Acts of 1939 and 1940 have been the ones chiefly involved in matters of ex post facto cases; but it should be emphasized again that these acts were emergency in nature and have expired. Orders issued under the authority of these acts were upheld in two murder cases[53]. This appears to be another example of the application of the Irish principle of parliamentary supremacy as expressed in the Constitution : 'Nothing in this Constitution shall be invoked to invalidate any law enacted by the Oireachtas which is expressed to be for the purpose of securing the public safety and the preservation of the State in time of war or armed rebellion, or to nullify any act done or purporting to be done in time of war or armed rebellion in pursuance of any such law . . . '[54]. This article is in effect a provision for a *pro tanto* suspension of the Constitution.

Article 40, Section 6, Sub-sections 1 and 2 guarantee freedom to citizens to express freely convictions, to assemble peacefully and without arms, and to form associations and unions. The exercise of these rights is made subject to 'public order and morality'; 'blasphemous, seditious, or indecent' matters are excluded from the guarantee, and meetings may be regulated or even prevented in the public interest. Finally, 'Laws regulating the manner in which the right of forming associations and unions and the right to free assembly may be exercised shall contain no political, religious or class discrimination'[55].

Once again there seems to have been only one Supreme Court case in which an act of the parliament (Oireachtas) has been declared void on the basis of this provision[56]. In that case the Trade Union Act of 1941 which regulated labor union internal organization and membership was challenged. The Court in an opinion by Judge Murnaghan held that the act violated the Constitution because it limited 'the right of the citizen to join one or more prescribed associations'.

Since laws existing at the time of the adoption of the Constitution remained in full force and effect except when inconsistent with the Constitution, the provisions of statutes prohibiting picketing or watching another's premises except as specified were held still applicable in another case[57]. The Court held that Article 40 does not protect picketing not excepted by statute, specifically the Trade Disputes Act of 1906.

On the question of the degree of force which police or military authorities may use in maintaining domestic peace, the Supreme Court upheld a decision of the High Court by Hanna J. that gun-fire can be used only when necessary as a last resort to preserve life.[58]

The 'right of association' which the Supreme Court of the United States has deduced from the First Amendment is expressly set forth in the Irish Constitution in Article 40, Section 6, as noted. However, by the terms of the Constitution, statutes may be enacted for the regulation and control of this right when in the public interest, and various statutes have been adopted in line with this, notably the Offences Against the State Act of 1939 and the Defence Act of 1954. These apply primarily to subversive and treasonable activities.

In addition to *National Union of Railwaymen* v. *Sullivan and Others*,[59] already mentioned, two other cases have been decided by the Supreme Court on the place of trade unions relative to this right of association. In *Tierney* v. *Amalgamated Society of Wood-workers*[60] the Court held that a trade union was not compelled to accept as a member any person who possesses the qualifications for membership set forth by the union. In *Educational Company of Ireland* v. *Fitzpatrick and Others*[61] a majority of the judges held that picketing in protest against the failure of some employees to join the union was pressure of a sort that interfered with their constitutional right to join or not to join an association.

Picketing is illegal unless there is a dispute as defined by the Trade Disputes Act of 1906 or other legislation. Picketing is watching and besetting. In *Educational Company* v. *Fitzpatrick*[62] there was a trade dispute but the Court held (affirming Budd J.) that the provisions of the Act could not be applied to coerce persons to join a union against their wills. Under the Constitution a citizen "may not be compelled to join any association or union against his will"[63].

As noted, the constitutional right of assembly[64] is specifically conditioned not only by the provision 'peaceably and without arms' but also by the additional statement that "Provision may be made by law to prevent or control meetings which are determined in accordance with law to be calculated to cause a breach of the peace or to be a danger or nuisance to the general public and to prevent or control meetings in the vicinity of either House of the Oireachtas"[65]. Statutes have prohibited assemblies in certain places[66]. Further, there are common law limitations on the right of assembly that are recognized. Any meeting of three or more persons which is likely to involve violence or a reasonable apprehension of violence is an unlawful assembly. As defined by McLoughlin J. (High Court) in *Barrett* v. *Tipperary* (*North Riding*) *County Council,*[68] "there must be at least three persons assembled and the conduct of the persons so assembled must be such as to afford evidence of force or violence in the commission of an offence or of some show of force or violence or of some breach of the peace or of some conduct tending to excite alarm in the mind of a person of firm and reasonable courage." Even lawful assemblies may be restrained or dispersed if necessary in order to prevent a breach of the peace[69].

Freedom of speech and press under Article 40 is again a conditioned guarantee since the Constitution specifically states that this "shall not be used to undermine public order or morality or the authority of the State"[70]. Under the Offences Against the State Act, 1939, there cannot be published or distributed any 'incriminating document', that is, one issued by an unlawful organization or appearing to aid and abet such an organization, any treasonable document that is, one relating directly or indirectly to the commission of treason, or a seditious document, one containing matter calculated or tending to undermine the public order or authority of the government or to question the legal status of the government or the military forces of the government. A newspaper letter, article, or contribution that does these things is specifically proscribed by this statute. Furthermore, mere possession of any of these documents is an offense.

Under a statute in effect from 1939 to 1946, when the Act expired (the Emergency Powers Act of 1939), during the period of World War II there was considerable censorship of the mails and newspapers and periodicals. During the entire existence of the Republic there has been in force an Official Secrets Act, the most recent having been adopted in 1963. This legislation has proscribed the communication of official information, without authority, that may be detrimental to the national security. There apparently has been no judicial consideration of the arrest and detention powers under the Act.

Publication of matter that is insulting to or abusive of courts or judges has on several occasions in recent years been held subject to contempt of court charges[71].

Blasphemy and obscenity are specifically prohibited by the Constitution[72]. However, there appears to have been only one prosecution under this subject, that for 'an indecent and profane performance' in a Dublin theatre[73]. In District Court the case was dismissed and no appeal was taken. There is an official Censor of Films and a Censorship of Film Appeals Board but no case involving such matters has come to the courts[74].

Under the Censorship of Publication Acts of 1929 and 1946 there is a Censorship of Publications Board and an Appeal Board to examine books published in Ireland or imported on which a complaint has been filed either by an official or by a private person. The Board on its own initiative may undertake an examination. Under the statute only the possible injury to public morals is to be considered. No action of the Board has ever been challenged in the courts.

Communications in the mails or by telegraph or telephone may be intercepted under a warrant issued on the personal authority of the Minister for Justice for reasons of national security or for detection or prevention of serious crime[75]. No court cases have been heard involving this and there appears to be no basis for challenging the practice under the Constitution[76].

In Ireland, radio and television are a government monopoly, Radio Telefís Eireann, under an Authority appointed for this purpose under the Broadcasting Authority Act of 1960. Under the Constitution the government is to see that broadcasting is not used "to undermine public order or morality or the authority of the State"[77].

Article 41, Section 1, Sub-section 1. The State recognizes the Family as the Natural primary and fundamental unit group of Society, and as a moral institution possessing inalienable and imprescriptible rights, antecedent and superior to all positive law.

Sub-section 2. The State, therefore, guarantees to protect the Family in its constitution and authority, as the necessary basis of social order and as indispensable to the welfare of the Nation and the State.

Section 2, Sub-section 1. In particular, the State recognizes that by her life within the home, woman gives to the State a support without which the common good cannot be achieved.

Sub-section 2. The State shall, therefore, endeavour to ensure that mothers shall not be obliged by economic necessity to engage in labour to the neglect of their duties in the home.

Section 3, Sub-section 1. The State pledges itself to guard with special care the institution of Marriage, on which the Family is founded, and to protect it against attack.

Sub-section 2. No law shall be enacted providing for the grant of a dissolution of marriage.

Sub-section 3. No person whose marriage has been dissolved under the civil law of any other State but is a subsisting valid marriage under the law for the time being in force within the jurisdiction of the Government and Parliament established by this Constitution shall be capable of contracting a valid marriage within that jurisdiction during the lifetime of the other party to the marriage so dissolved.

This Article and Article 42 are perhaps the most unique among the guarantees of the Irish 'Bill of Rights', not only because of the substance of the guarantees but also, by contrast with the other Irish guarantees, there is no provision for legislative suspension of the guarantees. However, Article 28, Section 3, Sub-section 3 would appear to allow for the 'suspension' of any constitutional right even though it might be difficult to assert that the suspending Act was 'for the purpose of securing the public safety' as provided in Article 28. In *Mayo-Perrott* v. *Mayo-Perrott*[78] the Supreme Court refused to enforce the judgment of an English court in a divorce case, holding that divorce is unknown to and prohibited by Irish law. This is a good example of the potential of judicial activity under this guarantee.

In husband and wife nullity suits this particular article of the Constitution has had no application[79]. In two cases involving separation deeds, Article 41, Section 3 was invoked but held to have no application[80].

Article 42, Section 1. The State acknowledges that the primary and natural educator of the child is the Family and guarantees to respect the inalienable right and duty of parents to provide, according to their means, for the religious and moral, intellectual, physical and social education of their children.

Section 2. Parents shall be free to provide this education in their homes or in private schools or in schools recognized or established by the State.

Section 3, Sub-section 1. The State shall not oblige parents in violation of their conscience and lawful preference to send their children to schools established by the State, or to any particular type of school designated by the State.

Sub-section 2. The State shall, however, as guardian of the common good, require in view of actual conditions that the children receive a certain minimum education, moral, intellectual and social.

Section 4. The State shall provide for free primary education and shall endeavour to supplement and give reasonable aid to private and corporate educational initiative, and, when the public good requires it, provide other educational facilities or institutions with due regard, however, for the rights of parents, especially in the matter of religious and moral formation.

Section 5. In exceptional cases, where the parents for physical or moral reasons fail in their duty towards their children, the State as guardian of the common good, by appropriate means shall endeavour to supply the place of the parents, but always with due regard for the natural and imprescriptible rights of the child.

In the interpretation of this provision of the Constitution the Supreme Court has held void a statute whose purpose was to give to the Minister for Education the final determination of which school (if any) children between the ages of six and fourteen should attend[81]. In other cases the question of the custody and the rearing of children has been decided in the light of Article 42, with the role of the parent emphasized[82].

One of the most famous, interesting and controversial cases to arise under this portion of the Constitution was *In re Tilson, Infants*[83] in which the custody of children was decided on the basis of an ante-nuptial agreement. The Court held that a joint agreement by the parents dealing with the religious upbringing of children was binding under Article 42, Section 1 of the Constitution. In another case, *In re Blake, decd.*[84], a legacy made on condition that the children of the deceased's daughter be reared as Catholics was voided as interfering with the right of parents to provide for the education, including religious education, of their children under this Article of the Constitution.

Article 43, Section 1, Sub-section 1. The State acknowledges that man, in virtue of his rational being, has the natural right, antecedent to positive law, to the private ownership of external goods.

Sub-section 2. The State accordingly guarantees to pass no law attempting to abolish the right of private ownership or the general right to transfer, bequeath, and inherit property.

Section 2, Sub-section 1. The State recognizes, however, that the exercise of the rights mentioned in the foregoing provisions of this Article ought, in civil society, to be regulated by the principles of social justice.

Sub-section 2. The State, accordingly, may as occasion requires delimit by law the exercise of the said rights with a view to reconciling their exercise with the exigencies of the common good.

This is another example of the tendency of the Irish Constitution to recognize a right but at the same time to acknowledge that the state may delimit by ordinary statutory law the exercise of such rights in order to care for 'the exigencies of the common good'[85]. In recent years there has been considerable legislation in the social and economic fields that could be interpreted as 'delimiting' the exercise of the right to private property. In only one case under the present Constitution has the Supreme Court held a statute void on the basis of incompatibility with this Article[86]. Here a statute had attempted to divert funds whose ownership was in doubt to a statutory board for a charitable purpose. In cases since then the Court has consistently held to the proposition that legislative discretion in the economic field should not be made the subject of judicial review[87].

In the first of these cases a statutory grant of power to the Irish Land Commission to recover possession of property previously allotted by the Commission was upheld and in the second case statutory provisions for the forfeiture of an automobile under a hire-purchase agreement was also upheld. Mention should also be made of *Pigs Marketing Board* v. *Donnelly (Dublin) Ltd.*[88] in which legislation passed to regulate the production and marketing of bacon and to authorize the Pigs Marketing Board to fix the price of pigs was upheld against the contention that it was contrary to Article 43. In his opinion Judge Hanna noted that 'the Oireachtas must be the judge of whatever limitation is to be enacted'.

Article 44, Section 1, Sub-section 1. The State acknowledges that the homage of public worship is due to Almighty God. It shall hold His Name in reverence, and shall respect and honour religion.

Sub-section 2. The State recognizes the special position of the Holy Catholic Apostolic and Roman Church as the guardian of the Faith professed by the great majority of the citizens.

Sub-section 3. The State also recognizes the Church of Ireland, the Presbyterian Church in Ireland, the Methodist Church in Ireland, the Religious Society of Friends in Ireland, as well as the Jewish Congregations and the other religious denominations existing in Ireland at the date of the coming into operation of this Constitution.

Section 2, Sub-section 1. Freedom of conscience and the free profession and practice of religion are, subject to public order and morality, guaranteed to every citizen.

Sub-section 2. The State guarantees not to endow any religion.

Sub-section 3. The State shall not impose any disabilities or make any discrimination on the ground of religious profession, belief or status.

Sub-section 4. Legislation providing State aid for schools shall not discriminate between schools under the management of different religious denominations, nor be such as to affect prejudicially the right of any child to attend a school receiving public money without attending religious instruction at that school.

Sub-section 5. Every religious denomination shall have the right to manage its own affairs, own, acquire and administer property, movable and immovable, and maintain institutions for religious or charitable purposes.

Sub-section 6. The property of any religious denomination or any educational institution shall not be diverted save for necessary works of public utility and on payment of compensation.

This Article guarantees freedom for all religious sects existing in Ireland at the time of the adoption of the Constitution as well as freedom of personal conscience in religious matters. State endowment of any religion is forbidden as well as discrimination in any way between schools of different religions including state aid for those schools. In practice there is separation of church and state even though the Roman Catholic Church is given 'special position' by the terms of the Constitution[89]. Religious discrimination is forbidden both by this Article and Article 40[90].

There has been no decision by the Supreme Court dealing with these provisions of the Constitution. This Article in the past has been considered rather incidentally in some cases before the High Court but not in an important way[91]. Very recently, however, Article 44 has been brought into issue in a case in which the validity of closing hours regulations for shops was challenged because they prescribed closing hours for food merchants but made an exception in favour of shops selling only meat killed by the Jewish ritual method. The High Court held this invalid as contrary to Article 44 as discrimination in favor of a particular section of the community and the Constitution forbids 'any discrimination on the ground of religious profession, belief or status'. The Supreme Court affirmed this judgment with an opinion by Mr. Justice Walsh[92].

In *The State (O'Connor)* v. *O Caomhanaigh*[93] the Supreme

Court in the only case of the kind since the adoption of the current Constitution in 1937 rejected the contention that in the light of Article 44 the Tumultuous Risings (Ireland) Act of 1831 could not be regarded as having been made subject to the continuation provisions of the Constitutions of 1922 and 1937[94] and made a part of the law of the land. The Court held that there was no religious discrimination in the statute itself and that the motives of those who enacted the statute could not be considered.

Article 45. The principles of social policy set forth in this Article are intended for the general guidance of the Oireachtas. The application of those principles in the making of laws shall be the care of the Oireachtas exclusively, and shall not be cognisable by any Court under any of the provisions of this Constitution.

Section 1. The State shall strive to promote the welfare of the whole people by securing and protecting as effectively as it may a social order in which justice and charity shall inform all the institutions of the national life.

Section 2. The State shall, in particular, direct its policy towards securing

i. That the citizens (all of whom, men and women equally, have the right to an adequate means of livelihood) may through their occupations find the means of making reasonable provision for their domestic needs.

ii. That the ownership and control of the material resources of the community may be so distributed amongst private individuals and the various classes as best to subserve the common good.

iii. That, especially, the operation of free competition shall not be allowed so to develop as to result in the concentration of the ownership or control of essential commodities in a few individuals to the common detriment.

iv. That in what pertains to the control of credit the constant and predominant aim shall be the welfare of the people as a whole.

v. That there may be established on the land in economic security as many families as in the circumstances shall be practicable.

Section 3, Sub-section 1. The State shall favour and, where necessary, supplement private initiative in industry and commerce.

Sub-section 2. The State shall endeavour to secure that private enterprise shall be so conducted as to ensure reasonable efficiency in the production and distribution of goods and as to protect the public against unjust exploitation.

Section 4, Sub-section 1. The State pledges itself to safeguard with especial care the economic interests of the weaker sections of the community, and, where necessary, to contribute to the support of the infirm, the widow, the orphan, and the aged.

Sub-section 2. The State shall endeavour to ensure that the strength and health of workers, men and women, and the tender age of children shall not be abused and that citizens shall not be forced by economic necessity to enter avocations unsuited to their sex, age or strength.

The heading of this Article, 'Directive Principles of Social Policy' indicates its general purpose. Here are set forth the ideals of social justice 'for the general guidance of the Oireachtas'. Furthermore, these provisions are not to be cognisable by any court under this Constitution. There is a finality about such phraseology, but what is excluded, in fact, is the application of those principles by the Court to legislation. If, for instance, the Court was considering the question of whether some provision of the common law was consistent with the Constitution, e.g. the principle which says that a man can beat his wife with a stick no wider than his little finger, the Court would surely be entitled to look at Article 45 to see if the common law principle was or was not consistent with the Constitution. Moreover, it may well be that in considering the constitutionality of a pre-1937 statute the Court would also be entitled to look at the directive principles of social policy[95].

REFERENCES

1. Irish Constitution, Art. 34 (3), (2). But see *The State (Sheerin)* v. *The Governor of St. Patrick's Institution and the Attorney General*, 1966 I.R. 379, which leaves open the possibility that the question whether a pre-1937 statute is or is not consistent with the Constitution may be raised in the District Court or the Circuit Court.
2. 6 George I, Chap. 5 (English), 1719.
3. Irish Free State Constitution, Art. 73.
4. Irish Constitution, Art. 50 (1), (2).
5. Irish Free State Constitution, Art. 73.
6. *The State (Nicolau)* v. *An Bord Uchtala*, 1966 I.R. 567.
7. Irish Constitution, Art. 40 (4), (2) and (3).
8. See Note 6, *supra*. See also *In re Philip Clarke* and Livestock Marts Act

Case (*East Donegal Cooperative Society, Ltd. and Others* v. *The Attorney General*, 1970 I.L.T.R. 81.

9. *In re Article* 26 *of the Constitution and the Offences Against the State (Amendment) Bill, 1940,* 1940 I.R. 470, 481.

10. 1958 I.R. 29.

11. *Macauley* v. *Minister for Posts and Telegraphs,* 1966 I.R. 345.

12. 1965 I.R. 294.

13. *In re Philip Clarke,* 1950 I.R. 235.

14. *The State (Burke)* v. *Lennon and Attorney General,* 1940 I.R. 136.

15. 1967 I.R. 147.

16. *The State (Dowling)* v. *Kingston,* 1937 I.R. 699.

17. 1965 I.R. 142.

18. See also Irish Constitution, Art. 28 (3), (3) and *The State (Walsh and Others)* v. *Lennon and Others,* 1942 I.R. 112.

19. See Health Act, 1947, Sects. 94 and 95.

20. *In re Article* 26 *of the Constitution and the Offences Against the State (Amendment) Bill, 1940,* 1940 I.R. 470.

21. See also Criminal Procedure Act, 1967.

22. *Conroy* v. *Attorney General and Another,* 1965 I.R. 411, a drunk driving case; *Melling* v. *O Mathghamhna,* 1962 I.R. 1, a smuggling case; *The State (Sheerin)* v. *Kennedy,* 1966 I.R. 379, a case under the Prevention of Crime Act, 1908, Sect. 2.

23. *Attorney General* v. *Henry White,* 1947 I.R. 247 and *Christie* v. *Leachinsky* [1947] Appeal Cases 573.

24. Offences Against the State (Amendment) Act, 1940, No. 2.

25. *Attorney General* v. *Coyne and Wallace,* 101 I.L.T.R. 17, 1963.

26. U.S. Constitution, Eighth Amendment. 'Excessive bail shall not be required . . .'

27. A case dealing with refusal of bail is *Attorney General* v. *Ball,* 1958 I.R. 280, 287. See also *The People* v. *O'Callaghan,* 1966 I.R. 501, 504.

28. Irish Constitution, Art. 40 (4), (3).

29. Convention, Art. 6 (3).

30. Irish Constitution, Art. 29 (6).

31. Criminal Justice (Legal Aid) Act, 1962.

32. *The State (Richard Tynan)* v. *Governor of Portlaoise Prison (re Michael Woods).* Decided December 19, 1967. Unreported.

33. Irish Constitution, Art. 38 (5). U.S. Constitution, Sixth Amendment.

34. Irish Constitution, Art. 38 (3, 4, 5).

35. See *Patton* v. *United States,* 281 U.S. 276, 1930; Juries Act, 1927 and Juries Act, 1945 (No. 24 of 1945), Sect. 6.

36. See Offences Against the State Act (No. 13 of 1939), 1939, especially Sect. 35.

37. Irish Constitution, Art. 34 (1).

38. Irish Constitution, Art. 38 (6).

39. Irish Constitution, Art. 38 (4).

40. See Criminal Justice Act, 1951, Sect. 20.1 and sub-sections 3 and 4. Under this statute a court could make an exception to public preliminary examination when 'expedient for the purpose of ensuring that the

accused will not be prejudiced in his trial'. See also Criminal Procedure Act, 1967, Sect. 16 amending Sect. 20 of 1951 Act. See also *In re Redbreast Preserving Co., Ltd.*, 91 I.L.T.R. 12, 1957.

41. Criminal Procedure Act, 1967 [No. 12 of 1967], Sect. 15.

42. See Offences Against the State Act, 1939 and 1940. See also Emergency Powers Act, 1939. This Act was temporary emergency legislation and has not been in force since 1946. See *The State (Walsh and Others)* v. *Lennon and Others*, 1942 I.R. 112, this case involving a charge of murder in connection with a conspiracy.

43. Criminal Justice Act, 1951, Sect. 3, Sub-section 3 (b).

44. Criminal Justice (Evidence) Act, 1924.

45. *Griffin* v. *California*, 380 U.S. 609, 1965.

46. See Emergency Powers Act of 1939, now expired, and Offences Against the State Act, 1939, Sect. 52. In this Act the Garda Siochana (the Irish Permanent police force) is given broad powers of arrest, search, and detention without warrant. See also *The People (Attorney General)* v. *Doyle and Maher*, 77 I.L.T.R. 108, 1943.

47. Irish Constitution, Art. 38 (1); Art. 40 (4), (1); Art. 40 (6), (6).

48. *In re Article 26 of the Constitution and the Offences Against the State (Amendment) Bill, 1940*, 1940 I.R. 470.

49. The presumption of constitutionality has another important effect as far as the judicial review of administrative action is concerned. If a post-1937 statute is capable of two interpretations, one of which is in accord with the Constitution and one of which violates the Constitution, the Supreme Court will presume that the Oireachtas intended only the constitutional interpretation. As a consequence, any administrative act which might nominally be held to be within one interpretation of the Act may be held to be unconstitutional and invalid. In this connection see *East Donegal Cooperative Society, Ltd. and Others* v. *The Attorney General*, 1970 I.L.T.R. 81, usually known as the Livestock Marts Act Case. This decision ruled a portion of the Livestock Marts Act, 1967, unconstitutional as violative of Article 40, Section 1, the provision dealing with equality before the law.

50. Interpretation Act, 1937, Section 14. See also *The People (Attorney General)* v. *Dermody*, 1956 I.R. 307; *Attorney General* v. *Mallen*, 1957 I.R. 344; and *The People (Attorney General)* v. *O'Brien*, 1963 I.R. 92; *The State (Walsh and Others)* v. *Lennon and Others*, 1942 I.R. 112.

51. *The State (Woods)* v. *The Governor of Mountjoy Prison*, 1962 I.R. 248.

52. *Calder* v. *Bull*, 3 Dallas 386, 1798.

53. *In re McGrath and Harte*, 1941 I.R. 68 and *The State (Walsh and Others)* v. *Lennon and Others*, 1942 I.R. 112.

54. Irish Constitution, Art. 28 (3), (3).

55. Irish Constitution, Art. 40 (6), (2).

56. *National Union of Railwaymen (NUR)* v. *Sullivan and Others*, 1947 I.R. 77.

57. *Brendan Dunne, Ltd.* v. *Fitzpatrick and Others*, 1958 I.R. 29.

58. In this case Judge Hanna had applied the opinion of Viscount Haldane in the Report of the Proceedings of the Select Committee on the Employ-

ment of Military in the Case of Disturbance (1908) and that of the Special Commissioners in the Report on the Bachelor's Walk Shooting (1914). *Lynch* v. *Fitzgerald* (No. 2), 1938 I.R. 382.

59. 1947 I.R. 77.
60. 1959 I.R. 254.
61. 1961 I.R. 370.
62. 1961 I.R. 345.
63. See *Dunne, Ltd.* v. *Fitzpatrick and Others*, 1958 I.R. 29. See also Electricity (Special Provisions) Act of 1966, Section 6 which specifically prohibits picketing in an industrial dispute.
64. Irish Constitution, Art. 40 (6), (1).
65. Irish Constitution, Art. 40 (6), (1, ii).
66. See, for example, Offences Against the State Act, 1939 (Leinster House).
67. 1964 I.R. 22.
68. 1964 I.R. 22.
69. *Humphries* v. *Connor*, 17 C.L.L.R. 1, 1864; *O'Kelly* v. *Harvey*, 14 L.R.Ir. 105, 1883; *Coyne* v. *Tweedy*, 2 I.R. 167, 1898.
70. Irish Constitution, Art. 40 (6), (1, i).
71. See, for example, *Attorney General* v. *O'Ryan and Boyd*, 1946 I.R. 70 (Circuit Court Judge); *Attorney General* v. *Connolly*, 1947 I.R. 213 (Special Criminal Court).
72. Irish Constitution, Art. 40 (6), (1, i).
73. The production was "The Rose Tattoo" by Tennessee Williams.
74. Film Censorship Acts of 1923, 1925, and 1930.
75. Post Office Act of 1908, Sect. 56.
76. John M. Kelly, *Fundamental Rights in the Irish Law and Constitution*, p. 140.
77. Irish Constitution, Art. 40 (6), (1, i).
78. 1958 I.R. 336.
79. See, for example, *Griffith* v. *Griffith*, 1944 I.R. 35.
80. *Lewis* v. *Lewis*, 1940 I.R. 42; *Ormsby* v. *Ormsby*, 79 I.L.T.R. 97.
81. *In re Article 26 and the School Attendance Bill*, 1942, 1943 I.R. 334. The legislation and the case were concerned also with the right of parents to provide for education in the home if they wished.
82. See, for example, *Burke and O'Reilly* v. *Burke and Quail*, 1951 I.R. 216; *In re O'Brien, an Infant*, 1954 I.R. 1; *In re Cullinane, an Infant*, 1954 I.R. 270; *In re Doyle, an Infant*, 1956 I.R. 217.
83. 1951 I.R. 1.
84. 1955 I.R. 89.
85. Irish Constitution, Art. 43 (2), (2).
86. *Buckley and Others (Sinn Fein)* v. *Attorney General and Another* (No. 1), 1950 I.R. 67.
87. See *Foley* v. *Irish Land Commission and Attorney General*, 1952 I.R. 118; *Attorney General* v. *Southern Industrial Trust and Simons*, 94 I.L.T.R. 161. See also Livestock Marts Act Case (*East Donegal Cooperative Society, Ltd. and Others* v. *The Attorney General*, 1970 I.L.T.R. 81) and the Town Planning Act Case (*Central Dublin Development Association, Ltd. and Others* v. *Attorney General*), decided by the High Court October

6, 1969, pending in the Supreme Court. This last-named case involves the Local Government Act, 1963.

88. 1939 I.R. 413.
89. Irish Constitution, Art. 44 (1), (2).
90. Irish Constitution, Art. 44 (2), (3); Art. 40 (6), (2).
91. See *Crichton and Others* v. *Irish Land Commission and Gault*, 84 I.L.T.R. 87; *Schlegel* v. *Corcoran and Gross*, 1942 I.R. 19; *Cook* v. *Carroll*, 1945 I.R. 515.
92. See *Quinn's Supermarket, Ltd.* v. *The Attorney General*, decided by the High Court July 1, 1968 (opinion by McLoughlin J.), and by the Supreme Court April 2, 1971. Irish Constitution, Art. 44 (2), (3).
93. 1963 I.R. 112.
94. Constitution of the Irish Free State, Art. 73. Irish Constitution, Art. 50.
95. This matter has been raised in *Gerald O'Brien* v. *Manufacturing Engineering, Ltd.*, decided by the High Court July 31, 1969, pending in the Supreme Court.

Note should be taken of the fact that two judgments of the Supreme Court of considerable constitutional importance were delivered during the Trinity Term, 1971. The first of these was *In The Matter of Padraic Haughey* in which the Court held that certain provisions of a statute were unconstitutional which allowed a person to be punished as if he had been guilty of contempt of court for failing to give evidence or refusing to answer questions before a parliamentary committee. The second case was that of *Byrne* v. *Ireland* in which the Court completely swept away the doctrine of sovereign immunity. The Court held that the State may be sued by name for the damage caused by the wrongful acts of any of its servants, officials, employees, etc. committed in the course of the exercise of their duties.

APPENDICES

The Judicial Oath

In the presence of Almighty God

I, ...

do solemnly and sincerely promise and declare that I will duly and faithfully and to the best of my knowledge and power execute the office of ....

without fear or favour, affection or ill-will towards any man, and that I will uphold the Constitution and the laws. May God direct and sustain me.

The Supreme Court

Judges of the Supreme Court since its establishment on 29 September 1961 under the Courts (Establishment and Constitution) Act, 1961.

	I.	II.	III.	IV.	V.
From 29. 9. 1961	Maguire C. J.	Lavery J.	Kingsmill Moore J.	O Dalaigh J.	Haugh J.
From 18. 12. 1961	O Dálaigh C. J.	Lavery J.	Kingsmill Moore J.	Haugh J.	Walsh J.
From 18. 3. 1965	O Dálaigh C. J.	Lavery J.	Haugh J.	Walsh J.	O'Keeffe J.
From 6. 10. 1966	O Dálaigh C. J.	Haugh J.	Walsh J.	Budd J.	Fitzgerald J.
From 2. 5. 1969	O Dálaigh C. J.	Walsh J.	Budd J.	Fitzgerald J.	McLoughlin J.

The Judges of Ireland

(At the time of this survey, 1969)

The Supreme Court:

The Hon Cearbhall O Dálaigh, Chief Justice
The Hon Mr Justice Brian Walsh
The Hon Mr Justice F. G. Budd
The Hon Mr Justice Wm. O'B. Fitzgerald
The Hon Mr Justice Richard McLoughlin

The High Court:

The Hon Mr Justice Andreas O'Keeffe, President of the High Court
The Hon Mr Justice George Murnaghan
The Hon Mr Justice Thomas Teevan
The Hon Mr Justice John Kenny
The Hon Mr Justice Seamus Henchy
The Hon Mr Justice Sean Butler
The Hon Mr Justice Denis Pringle

Ex officio:

The Hon Mr Justice Barra O Briain, President of the Circuit Court

The Circuit Court:

The Hon Mr Justice Barra O Briain, President of the Circuit Court
His Honour Judge J. C. Conroy
His Honour Judge John James Durcan
His Honour Judge Thomas J. Neylon
His Honour Judge Kenneth Deale
His Honour Judge Sean MacD. Fawsitt
His Honour Judge James S. McGivern
His Honour Judge P. Noel Ryan
His Honour Judge Conor Maguire
His Honour Judge Herbert Wellwood

The District Court:
Cathal O Floinn, President of the District Court
John Carr
Miss Eileen Kennedy
Walter H. Molony
Sean O Fearghail
P. D. O'Grady
Desmond O'Hagan
Riobard O hUadhaigh
A. A. Rochford
Michael Larkin
John Hugh Barry
Hugh C. McGahon
James P. Gilvarry
Samuel J. Shaw
Dermot Dunleavy
Thomas G. A. Burke
Joseph Michael MacGrath
James J. Sheerin
Donnchadh Ua Donnchada
Louis C. Murphy
Gordon J. Hurley
M. Cyril Maguire
Muirceartach E. de Burca
William Sweetman
M. J. C. Keane
John B. Farrell
Michael J. O'Hara
Denis O'Donovan
Kevin I. McCourt
Leo B. Skinner
John R. C. Coghlan
Arthur Lanigan O'Keeffe
John J. Delap
T. F. Donnelly
Herman Good

Retired Members:
Conor A. Maguire, former Chief Justice
James Murnaghan, former Judge of the Supreme Court
T. C. Kingsmill Moore, former Judge of the Supreme Court
Cahir Davitt, former President of the High Court

Deceased:
Kevin Haugh, former Judge of the Supreme Court

Annual Salaries of Judges

(Act No. 21 of 1968)

	£
Chief Justice	8000
President of the High Court	7000
Ordinary Judges of Supreme Court	7000
Ordinary Judges of High Court	6000
President of the Circuit Court	6000
Ordinary Judges of Circuit Court	5000
President of the District Court	4500
Other Justices of District Court	3750

SELECTED REFERENCES

Ball, F. Elrington. *The Judges in Ireland*, 1911-1921. (Two volumes, 1927.)

Barrington, Donal. "The Irish Constitution", *Irish Monthly*, Vols. 80 and 81.

Beth, Loren P. *The Development of Judicial Review in Ireland*, 1937-1966 (1967).

Bunreacht Na hEireann (Constitution of Ireland).

Chubb, Basil. *A Source Book of Irish Government* (1964).

The Constitution, Rules and Regulations of the General Council of the Bar of Ireland (1948).

Coogan, T. P. *Ireland Since the Rising* (1966).

Costello, Declan. "The Natural Law and the Irish Constitution", *Studies*, 1956.

Delany, V. T. H. *The Administration of Justice in Ireland* (1970).

Donaldson, Alfred Gaston. *Some Comparative Aspects of Irish Law* (1957).

Figgs, Darrell. *The Irish Constitution* (1922).

Gray, Tony. *The Irish Answer* (1966).

Harrison, Reginald A. *Law Reports*, 1939-1958.

The Incorporated Law Society of Ireland, Members' Handbook (1968).

Index of *Irish Law Times*.

Index of *Irish Reports*.

Index of *Northern Ireland Legal Quarterly*.

Index of *Solicitors Journal*.

Kelly, J. M. *Fundamental Rights in the Irish Law and Constitution* (1967).

McWhinney, Edward. *Judicial Review in the English Speaking World*. Chapter on Ireland (1960).

O'Donnell, James D. *How Ireland is Governed* (1970).

Index